# SOUTHERN AFRICAN
# I N S E C T S
## AND THEIR WORLD

A l a n    W e a v i n g

Struik Publishers (Pty) Ltd
(A member of Struik New Holland Publishing (Pty) Ltd)
Cornelis Struik House
80 McKenzie Street
Cape Town 8001

Reg. No 54/00965/07

2  4  6  8  10  9  7  5  3  1

First published in 2000

Managing editor: Simon Pooley
Editor: Peter Joyce
Designer: Dominic Robson
Cover design: Daniël Jansen van Vuuren
Proofreader: Thea Grobbelaar
Indexer: Brenda Brickman

Reproduction by Hirt & Carter (Pty) Ltd, Cape Town
Printed and bound by CTP Book Printers, Parow

ISBN 1 86872 320 8

*Front cover*, main picture: The emperor moth caterpillar; bottom row, left to right: Fruit chafer; grasshopper; ladybird; pollen wasp at the turretted entrance to its nest; shield bug nymphs; mating welwitschia bugs. *Back cover*, top to bottom: Satyrid butterfly; dragonfly laying eggs. *Title page:* Tachinid fly. *Opposite:* Emperor moth caterpillar.

# ACKNOWLEDGEMENTS

I am especially grateful to Professor Pat Hulley of Rhodes University for critically reading, and improving, the manuscript. Grateful thanks are also due to the following for their time, knowledge, and expertise in identifying insect specimens: Dr 'Chuck' Bellamy; the late Dr Sebastian Endrody-Younga; Dr Martin Kruger (Transvaal Museum); Dr Hamish Robertson (South African Museum); Dr Mervyn Mansell; Riaan Stals; Michael Stiller (National Collection of Insects); Dr Jason Londt (Natal Museum); Professor Denis Brothers (University of Natal); Dr Fred Gess (Albany Museum); Dr Tanza Crouch (Durban Natural Science Museum); Dr Eugene Marais (National Museum of Namibia), and Patrick Reavell (University of Zululand). I am indebted to Dr Fred Gess (Albany Museum) for the loan of specimens, and for allowing me free access to material and the entomology library, and to Dr Ferdie de Moore, also of the Albany Museum, for the loan of material.

I would also like to thank my daughter, Clare, and her husband, Darryn Chase, for live specimens of Parktown prawns; Mary Bursey of the East London Museum for a live flower mantid (*Pseudocreobotra wahlbergi*); Sarah Gess, Mike Picker and Hamish Robertson for the loan of slides, and Gerhard Marx for colour artwork. I am most grateful to Pippa Parker and the editorial staff of Struik Publishers for their help and encouragement.

*Alan Weaving*

# CONTENTS

# INTRODUCING INSECTS

'The only good insect is a dead one!' Sadly, such is the view of many people. Too often an encounter with an insect results in its untimely and violent end – and a quite unnecessary one, for these mostly harmless creatures play an honoured, and crucial, role in the natural scheme of things.

Having said that, though, there are indeed many insects that attract man's displeasure, and not without good reason. At home cockroaches infest our kitchens; fishmoths chew holes in papers and destroy book bindings; termites destroy wooden structures; timber beetles bore into furniture and roof beams; carpet beetles and clothes moths attack woollen rugs and garments; various beetles and moths infest cereals and flour.

A daunting array of insects ravages our gardens. Each year, millions of rands' worth of damage is done to commercial crops, and huge sums are spent trying to prevent or eradicate the infestations, an ongoing battle that sustains major chemical and equipment industries.

**Left:** The elegant grasshopper, *Zonocerus elegans*: a common southern African insect. **Above right:** The colourful caterpillar of the moth *Pseudaphelia apollinaris*. **Above:** The lovely painted lady is a cosmopolitan butterfly.

Blood-sucking insects such as mosquitoes, tsetse flies, biting midges, horseflies and fleas cause acute discomfort to man and his domestic animals, at worst spreading potentially fatal illnesses such as malaria and sleeping sickness.

With so much incriminating evidence one could perhaps be forgiven for dismissing all insects as undesirable, worthy only of extermination. The truth, though, is that this array of harmful creatures, large as it may seem, is an insignificant proportion of the multitude of insect species that inhabit our world, most of which have little or no direct impact on humankind. Moreover, an impressive number of them can and do help us. Indeed some of them are invaluable, if not essential, to our wellbeing. Many parasitic and predatory insects, notably some of the wasps, keep pests in check, and farmers depend on their help more and more as pest species build up resistance to commercial chemicals or, as in many cases, when it becomes impracticable or environmentally undesirable to use pesticides.

Some attempts at biological control (by natural means) have been especially successful. The release of egg parasitoids, tiny wasps that lay their eggs inside those of their hosts, has saved the timber industry huge sums of money by controlling the snout beetles and tortoise beetles that attack eucalyptus plantations. A minute parasitic wasp (*Aphelinus mali*) is employed against woolly aphids that invade apple orchards. The familiar Australian bug, a citrus pest, is controlled by a predatory ladybird (*Rodolia cardinalis*) introduced from Australia. In many places, exotic plants have become harmful weeds and, again, various insects have been harnessed to help check them. For instance cochineal insects and prickly pear moths (both natives to South America) have, between them, freed large areas of agricultural land from dense infestations of prickly pear.

Then there are those invaluable insects whose activities go largely unnoticed and unappreciated, most notably the pollinators on which the yield and quality of many crops are dependent. The honeybee is an obvious example, but only one of many: some of the flies, beetles, wasps, butterflies, moths and different kinds of bee play a vital role in pollination. Others supply food directly to man, among them termites, locusts, ants, stinkbugs and caterpillars. In southern Africa, the caterpillars of some emperor moths, and especially the mopane moth, are eaten by the local rural people, even canned for sale. Others provide honey, wax and silk. The larvae of certain leaf-eating beetles of the family Chrysomelidae are the source of a virulent poison which the traditional Bushman hunters apply to their arrow-tips.

Natural waste disposal is another important service. Termites and various beetle larvae break down leaf litter. Dead wood decomposes with the help of the larvae of goat moths, long-horned beetles, jewel beetles, various wood-borers and, of course, termites. Maggots of blowflies and flesh flies and the larvae of some beetles play a vital role in disposal of carrion. Incidentally, too, these insects even help police in their murder investigations: the size and age of fly maggots recovered from a corpse are pointers to the time of death. The part played by dung beetles in the disposing of waste matter is almost too well known to mention.

The introduced Australian bug *Icerya purchasi* can be controlled by a predatory ladybird.

Mopane worms serve as a valuable food source for rural folk.

## Insects in context

Insects are by far the most abundant of earth's life forms; no other group of animals is so much a part of everyday human existence. Yet many people do not know what an insect actually is. Nor can they readily distinguish between insects and other members of the great phylum Arthropoda (see box, pages 8–9).

This ignorance is due partly to the difficulty one has in empathizing with creatures that are so alien in looks and behaviour. But, in southern Africa especially, it can also be blamed on the glaring lack of popular books on the subject. This volume will hopefully go some way towards filling the gap. The great thing about insects is their accessibility – they occur everywhere. The excitement of the hunt, the discovery of yet another amazing example of camouflage or deception, need not wait for your next visit to a game reserve: there's variety enough, even drama in miniature, and of course plenty of fascination, in your own garden.

**Above:** The massive, fully grown larva of the msasa borer. **Right:** Larvae of jewel beetles also help dispose of wood waste; pictured is a mating pair of adults.

An impartial look at insects thus shows them in a much better light. The relatively few harmful species should not be allowed to deprive us of the great benefits, and the interest and enjoyment, the majority provide. And indeed of their charm: butterflies, moths, even many of the beetles, have undeniable aesthetic appeal. Other insect groups have few claims to beauty, but what they lack in terms of looks they more than make up for with their intriguing habits.

Carrion beetles provide an efficient clean-up service by breaking down carcasses.

*Sternocera orissa*, a large jewel beetle whose larvae play a useful part in wood decomposition.

These wasps (above and below) are clearly insects.

Spiders are arachnids, not insects.

## INSECTS AND OTHER ARTHROPODS: TELLING THE DIFFERENCE

The phylum Arthropoda, which means lite-rally 'joint-footed', contains many creatures besides insects, including spiders, scorpions, mites and ticks (Arachnida), millipedes (Diplopoda), cen-tipedes (Chilopoda), crabs, lobsters and bar-nacles (Crustacea).

All arthropods have a hard out-side skeleton. Their bodies are divided into segments, and are equipped with a number of appendages, including jointed legs, external sex organs,

antennae or feelers, and various components of the mouthparts such as mandibles, maxillae ('jaws') and chelicerae (food-catching claws).

**Insects**, though, are easily distinguishable from all other arthropods by the three sections into which their bodies are divided – head, thorax and abdomen. They have six jointed legs and, usually, four membranous wings (see pages 14–21 for more details). However, the young of some insects – caterpillars and mag-gots for example – look completely different from the adults.

**Spiders** and **scorpions** belong to the class Arachnida, in which the body has only two sections: the cephalothorax (combined

The scorpion also belongs to the class Arachnida.

The arachnids include red velvet mites.

Millipedes: class Diplopoda.

Centipedes: class Chilopoda.

head and thorax) and abdomen. Arachnids typically have six pairs of jointed appendages, the front pair forming jaws or fangs, the second pedipalps or pincers. The remaining four pairs are legs, the eight legs characterizing the class. **Ticks** and **mites** are also arachnids. Apart from some mites, they all have sucking mouthparts and four pairs of legs. Ticks are external, blood-sucking parasites that attach themselves to reptiles, birds and mammals. Mites are usually very small, feeding on plants, preying on small arthropods or living as external parasites on various animals.

Apart from a distinct head, **millipedes** and **centipedes** have no major subdivisions of the body. They are long and many-segmented. Millipedes are cylindrical with two pairs of legs per segment; centipedes are flattened and with one pair per segment. Millipedes scavenge and feed on vegetable matter; centipedes are carnivorous.

**Crustaceans** vary enormously in form, size and habitat; many are marine creatures, among which crabs and prawns are probably the most familiar. The head and thorax, like those of the arachnids, are fused. The abdomen is segmented. Every segment of the body has a pair of appendages modified for special purposes – for feeding, breathing, walking, swimming or grasping. Crustaceans normally have five pairs of legs but woodlice, one of the few terrestrial groups (commonly found in the garden and often confused with insects), have seven pairs.

Crabs: class Crustacea.

Woodlice: class Crustacea

Tailor ants use spun silk, provided by the larvae, to create the colony's nest.

Monkey beetles tunnel into composite flowers to feed, often mating in the process.

## The region's insect life

Southern Africa forms part of the sub-Saharan (also known as Afrotropical) zoogeographic region. It embraces a great variety of habitats, ranging from pure desert to moist savanna and subtropical forest, with intervening arid savanna, karoo, grassland, fynbos and montane forest. Over half the region is arid, the moister habitats confined to the eastern part of the subcontinent (forest, woodland and bushveld) and the south-western Cape (fynbos). This spectacular habitat diversity is reflected in an insect fauna that comprises at least 80 000 species.

A notable feature of the region is the narrow corridor of forest and woodland that extends northeastwards from Port Elizabeth and links up with larger areas of comparable habitat far to the north, in tropical Africa. This corridor allows many tropical species to extend their range much farther south than would otherwise be possible. Many of the insects found in this corridor are the same as, or very similar to, those occurring in East and even West Africa. Typical of these are butterflies such as the mocker swallowtail *Papilio dardanus*, the green-veined charaxes *Charaxes candiope* and many praying mantids. The tailor ant, with its amazing nest of leaves bound together with spun silk provided by its grubs, is a further reminder of this region's link with the tropics.

On the other hand, many of our insects are highly adaptable and range over the whole of sub-Saharan Africa with little regard to habitat type. A few among thousands of such species are the gaily-coloured elegant grasshopper which one meets in just about any place where there is some vegetation; the familiar black-and-yellow mud-dauber wasp; the large brown mason wasp; and, among the butterflies, the citrus swallowtail, the African monarch and the painted lady, all of which seem as much at home in the arid wastes of the Kalahari as in the eastern tropical corridor. The convolvulus hawk moth and silver-striped hawk moth are attracted to lights almost anywhere; the American bollworm shows up as a pest in gardens, vegetable patches and fruit orchards from Knysna to Nairobi. The rhinoceros beetle breeds in compost heaps everywhere.

The pale, wingless dune cricket of the genus *Comicus* is nocturnal, and well adapted to desert life.

Southern African insect life does, however, boast a number of characteristic and some unique species, many from the southwestern Cape and the drier western areas. Furry monkey beetles (tribe Hopliini), conspicuous and colourful visitors to flowers, are especially plentiful in the northwestern Cape (Namaqualand) and the Great Karoo. The Cape is home to the greatest variety of yellow-and-black (or yellow-and-brown) pollen wasps, another family of flower visitors. Thread-winged lacewings (family Nemopteridae), with their greatly elongated, ribbon-like hindwings, are among the more strikingly distinctive southern African insects.

You'll find a fascinating array of endemic desert specials in the sand dunes and stony gravel plains of the Namib. Among these are numerous tenebrionid beetles (see box), a few scarabaeid beetles and the pale, wingless, nocturnal dune crickets, all of which have adapted quite remarkably to the rigours of desert life.

Farther to the east, where the desert gives way to the better-vegetated Karoo and Kalahari regions – this is known as the central arid savanna zone – you'll find a wide range of flightless ground-living beetles. Most of these are tenebrionids, notably the familiar ground-tapping tok-tokkies and the heavily armoured lily weevils.

## BEETLES OF THE NAMIB

The Namib Desert is renowned for, among other things, the remarkable ways in which its tenebrionid beetles (the name means dark-coloured) have adapted to survive the high temperatures, the scarcity of food and the extreme dryness of their environment.

**Keeping cool** Many tenbebrionids are diurnal (daytime) species, but they confine their activities to the earlier part of the morning and later in the afternoon. During the hottest hours they bury themselves below the sand surface, where temperatures are significantly lower. Some minimize their exposure to intense heat by sprinting from one patch of shade to another with astonishing speed; others have ultra-long legs, which enable them to raise their bodies above the burning sand.

**Avoiding water loss** Dehydration through the spiracles (small openings that serve as air passages) is a major threat to desert-living insects. Tenebrionids have sacrificed the power of flight to overcome this: their fore-wings (elytra) are fused together, creating a protected cavity into which the abdominal spiracles open. This is perhaps the most effective of the adaptations. Water loss is further minimized, in some species, by a waxy layer covering the insect's cuticle.

**Finding food** Tenebrionids feed largely on the plant and animal detritus (debris) that accumulates on dune slipfaces, at the bases of grass tufts or around stones. To digest the plant detritus the insect needs to break down cellulose, and many species produce their own special enzymes (cellulases) for this purpose. The beetles' ability to use this abundant resource creates many food chains and so contributes handsomely to the great diversity of life in the Namib dunelands.

**Taking a drink** In the desert, water is a scarce resource. In places, however, certain beetles are able to exploit the fogs that often sweep in from the sea. Some such species face the incoming mist and take up a head-down stance known as 'fog-basking'. The moisture condenses on the beetle's body and trickles down to its mouthparts. Other species make trenches in the sand at right angles to the flow of the moisture-laden air and drink the water that collects.

Also common are tiger beetles and some striking carabids, the 'cheetahs of the insect world' which rely on speed for running down their prey. Here, too, there are some extraordinarily well-camouflaged endemic toad grasshoppers of the family Pamphagidae. Similar-looking species of the family Lathiceridae occur only in the region between the Orange River and southern Angola. The remarkable resemblance these grasshoppers bear to stones makes them almost invisible in their natural, stony habitat.

Other members of the Orthoptera group characteristic of southern Africa include the engagingly ugly armoured ground crickets (Hetrodinae), which are especially abundant in the Kalahari and Karoo, and whose populations sometimes reach almost plague proportions. At these times they can be seen in vast numbers scavenging dead animal or plant remains along the roads. No less than ten of the 12 genera of king crickets, which include the well-known Parktown prawn, are confined to southern Africa, occurring in moister eastern areas of the highveld and the tropical corridor (see page 10). The spectacularly inflated bladder grasshoppers are restricted to South Africa and occur only along the Cape and KwaZulu-Natal coastal belt except for one genus, *Physophorina*, which extends into East Africa.

Almost half the 820 or so species of butterfly in southern Africa are blues and coppers of the family Lycaenidae. The Cape fynbos is particularly rich in endemic species of this family as well as the family Satyridae. There are also some very distinctive flies (Diptera) with extraordinarily long proboscies (mouthparts) that enable them to suck nectar from the tubular (and often very lovely) flowers that are common in the region.

Most intriguing of all are some of the insects that are confined to the Cape Fold mountain belt, among them the unusually bulky Cape mountain cockroach. Especially interesting are those insects descended from ancient, primitive species and not found anywhere else in sub-Saharan Africa,

**Above and below:** The silver ghost moth, *Leto venus*, ranks among the most beautiful of southern Africa's palaeogenic, or ancient, insect species.

whose closest relatives are to be found elsewhere only in the southern parts of South America, Australia, and to a lesser extent in New Zealand. They are known as palaeogenic insects, and their curious distribution pattern is evidence that the land masses were once joined together, forming the ancient continent of Gondwanaland.

Stag beetles of the endemic genus *Colophon* are a good example. Fourteen species are confined to high mountain-tops in various parts of the southwestern and southern Cape, but have cousins in Australia and South America. Among the most interesting of our palaeogenic species is the long-legged, golden-haired cave cricket, *Speleiacris tabulae*, the only African representative of the camel crickets and found in just a few caves near Cape Town; other members of its subfamily occur only on the southern tip of South America, in the Falkland Islands, New Zealand and in southeastern Australia.

# THE LONG AND SHORT OF IT

According to some estimates there are between 15 and 30 million different insect species world-wide, of which about 750 000 are known to us, and some 80 000 are found in southern Africa. Indeed they make up a major portion of the global biomass – the total weight of all the earth's living organisms, plant and animal. At any given time, the weight of all the insects in the world would amount to about a trillion kilograms, exceeding that of all humanity. And they are amazingly diverse in their size, form, habit and habitat. Some of the extremes found in southern Africa are:

**Biggest** Stick insects hold the record, some reaching 250 mm in length.

**Heaviest** Longicorn beetles of the genus *Acanthophorus* can be three or four times heavier than the largest stick insects.

**Above:** The toad grasshopper resembles the stones among which it lives; only movement will reveal its presence. **Below left:** Longicorn beetles are among the heaviest of all insects. This is a msasa borer.

**Smallest** 'Fairy flies', minute wasps, are as little as 0,2 mm in length.

**Fastest** Some insects show an astonishing turn of speed. In the Namib Desert, a tenebrionid beetle species, *Onymacris plana*, holds the ground record, running across the hot sand at speeds of 1,15 metres per second (4,14 km/h). In the air, a number of wasps and bees can reach speeds of around 70 km/h – an incredible feat considering their size.

**Most dangerous to humans** In macro terms, undoubtedly the malarial anopheline mosquitoes. Honeybees are also dangerous: angry swarms can kill.

**Most deceitful** Insects are masters of deceit and camouflage. Several species of blue butterflies (Lycaenidae) flaunt false antennae and eyes at the tips of their hindwings, drawing the attention of predators away from their more vulnerable bodies. Toad grasshoppers are so like the stones they live among that they are virtually impossible to discern unless they move.

Insects are also renowned for their mimicry. For example, the females of the diadem butterfly *Hypolimnas misippus*, of the family Nymphalidae, disguise themselves as one or another of several distasteful or poisonous species of the butterfly family Danaidae, so that predators will leave them alone. One curious result of this mimicry is that female members of the same species look quite different from each other.

**Most colourful** Probably the moth known as the pleasant hornet (*Euchromia amoena*).

**Longest lived** Some of the free-roaming large lily weevils can live up to 30 years. The life spans of termite queens average six to nine years but can be as long as 50 years.

**Shortest lived** Many mayflies die within 24 hours of emerging from their nymphal skins.

**Most fertile** A queen *Macrotermes natalensis* termite can lay 30 000 eggs in a day, which amounts to an incredible 10 million in a year or 100 million during her lifetime. One oriental species has been reported to lay 86 400 eggs in a single day!

# INSECT BODIES

A careful search under rotting logs in the forests east of the Great Escarpment or south of the Cape Fold mountain belt might well yield one of the descendants of an extremely ancient group of animals. This is an onycophoran, a strange, soft-bodied, velvety creature that looks somewhat like a caterpillar and is the most primitive of all arthropods. What makes it especially interesting is that, although it derives from the segmented worms (phylum Annelida), it also represents the ancestral lineage that gave rise to the insects.

If you do come across an onycophoran, it is best to leave it alone: it will quickly die from moisture loss if not kept at a high humidity level. Moreover, the very survival of its kind is threatened by habitat destruction.

## Origins and evolution

The earliest insects were flightless, but the development of wings – the first of three major steps in insect evolution – was not long in coming. These were of the type that, like those of the modern dragonflies, could not be folded away (this is called 'palaeopterous'). Insects with such wings are accomplished fliers, but they are also at a disadvantage because the wings prevent them from hiding away under objects or in holes and crevices.

The second evolutionary step overcame this problem: the wings could now be folded back over the abdomen when not in use (neopterous). The young of the first neopterous insects looked and fed like the adults except that they were smaller and had no wings (hemimetabolous). Modern bugs and grasshoppers fall into this category.

The third and final major evolutionary change was the appearance of a more complicated life history, one in which the young pass through larval and pupal stages and do not look or behave in the least like the adults (holometabolous). Modern examples are the butterflies, the true flies, the beetles and the wasps. All these processes were finished and complete some 250 million years ago, and there have been no more physical evolutionary changes of comparable importance since then. Insects have therefore had a long time to evolve their incredible diversity, and to become the most abundant and successful form of life on earth.

However, there was one particularly significant development that did take place during the past 250 million years: social insects made their appearance. Among these are all the termites and ants and some of the bees and wasps (many others still live solitary lives).

Insect societies are not simple aggregations of more or less similar individuals who have 'chosen' to live together, as many mammals have done. Rather, they are for the most part highly complex communities of thousands, hundreds of thousands or, sometimes, more than a million insects, each one the offspring of a single queen. A colony is therefore one large family. Moreover, each family member is an incomplete animal in the sense that it cannot live independently.

**Left:** The patterns of butterfly and moth wings are created by a vast number of tiny overlapping scales.
**Above:** The structure of a dragonfly's wings is ancient in origin. **Top:** A cuckoo wasp. Light diffraction, from the sculptured surface of the cuticle, produces the insect's bright metallic hue.

## THE WONDER SUBSTANCE

Chitin, the material from which an insect's protective outer casing is made, is remarkably versatile. When combined with certain other substances it takes on special properties: hardness for example, or the ability to allow liquids and gases to pass through. Its waxy outer layer keeps the insect body from drying out. It can also be made hard enough for the tough, sharp, cutting edges of mandibles, or the points of sharp stings. In a less modified, more flexible form it serves as the soft joints between the armour plates. In yet other combinations it is used in the construction of the sense organs, even the lenses of the eyes.

This all-purpose material can be manipulated in endless ways to provide the body with nodules, tubercles, spines or horns, so enabling the insect world to develop its enormous range of body shapes. Bodies are often

Pigments in the cuticle endow this blister beetle with its distinctive colours.

clothed in a variety of hairs or scales (setae), all made from chitin and connected to the cuticle via a flexible joint. Among the various setae are many that are sensitive to touch, or can sense vibrations. The hairs on stinging caterpillars are hollow setae with poison glands at their bases. The colours of insects are due either to pigments in the chitin or the sculpting of its surface to create light diffraction.

---

Every member of an insect society has specific duties. Different tasks may prompt special modifications to the body, which sometimes result in the development of strikingly different looking individuals (castes) within the same colony – as in the termites and ants. The organization of the community, the way it works, has often been compared with that of an individual mammal's living body. The reproductive organs of the animal, for example, are represented by the queen and males of the colony, the various tissues (heart, brain, gut and so forth) by the workers, and the circulation of blood and lymph by the exchange of food between the colony's members. Thinking along these lines, it is not difficult to view a column of army ants as a single, large, relentless predator as it kills and devours every living creature in its path. Similarly, the functioning of a termite colony can be likened to that of the body of an antelope or other large herbivore (both are vegetarian).

Because insect colonies behave as units, grow and reproduce themselves by founding new colonies, and are organized into castes, the colony can be regarded as more than the sum of

its parts. It is the whole colony, not just the individual members, which grows, adapts, survives. This creates the concept of the 'superorganism'.

## Structure and function

Insects differ in a major way from vertebrate animals in their external skeleton – a rigid outer casing known as the cuticle. The casing can be likened to a suit of armour, and indeed, like the latter, it comprises a series of articulating plates to provide flexibility of movement. However, it is made from a substance called chitin (see box above), a much superior and more mouldable material than metal. Chitin combines great strength with lightness, which is essential for flight.

The top or back of an insect is referred to as being dorsal and the underneath or front as ventral. The head is usually quite distinct, and is equipped with a pair of antennae, often referred to as 'feelers', which are sensitive to touch and smell. There is also a set of mouthparts, variously modified for different diets and methods of feeding, namely biting and chewing (mandibulate) or piercing and/or sucking (see opposite).

# INSECT MOUTHPARTS

Grasshopper: the mouthparts are adapted for chewing vegetation.

Assassin bugs are armed with sharp, curved probosces for piercing the bodies of their prey.

The hawk moth caterpillar chews leaves.

This carabid beetle has powerful mandibles.

Plant bugs pierce vegetable tissue with slender probosces and suck up the sap.

Blowflies have lapping mouthparts that are designed to suck up liquids.

Nectar-feeding insects boast unusually long probosces for probing flowers.

The predatory robber fly stabs and sucks with its stiletto-like proboscis.

# THE WINGS: VARIATIONS ON A THEME

The differences in the design and configuration of insect wings are considerable. Indeed, some groups can be identified by their wings alone.

Flies have no hindwings (3): what's left of them are reduced to tiny, club-shaped balancing organs known as halteres. The forewings of stick insects (1) and earwigs (12) are much reduced, and in the latter serve as covers for the intricately folded hindwings. Some groups, such as cockroaches (7), praying mantids and grasshoppers (4) have the forewings thickened to act as protective covers to the hindwings when folded. This is carried to the extreme in beetles (10), in which the forewings no longer take an active part in flight. Bugs of the suborder Heteroptera (11) have only the basal, or inner, half of the forewing thickened. And even in those groups which have all four wings uniformly membranous (2,5,6,8,9 and 13), each can still be recognized from its wing shape and the patterns of the wing veins. All winged ants, bees and wasps, and some butterflies, moths and caddisflies, link the fore- and hindwings together with hooks or bristles for better flight control.

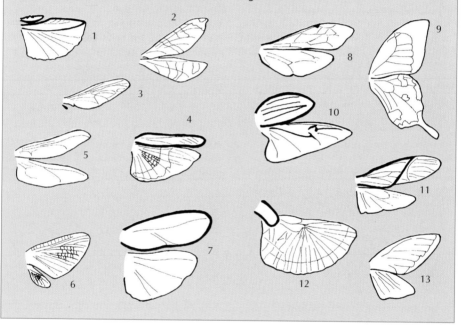

Insects have two types of eyes: a pair of large multifaceted compound eyes and, often, three (sometimes one, sometimes two) simple eyes (ocelli) in between. The latter are equipped with lenses but are more suitable for sensing changes in light intensity than for seeing objects. Compound eyes on the other hand are remarkable structures, quite unlike the eyes of vertebrates. They are especially well designed for seeing rapid movement and estimating distance, hence the consummate ease with which many insects escape capture. They are made up of hundreds or even thousands of individual facets, each consisting of a lens and an independent nerve connection to the brain. An insect's eyes are also sensitive to the plane of polarized light, which it uses, often in quite remarkable fashion, as a navigational aid.

**Above and right:** Insects have compound eyes between which are (in many cases) three simple eyes.

The three-segmented thorax has three pairs of legs (one pair per segment) and two pairs of wings (one pair each on the second and third segment). Each leg consists of a femur, a tibia and a tarsus with up to six joints and usually ending in a pair of claws. Two normally inconspicuous segments (coxa and trochanter) articulate the leg with the body. The wings may be modified in various ways, especially the front pair, and the hind pair may be absent as in the true flies (Diptera). Much of the thorax is occupied by muscles needed to operate the legs and wings.

The abdomen has up to eleven segments, sometimes as few as three, each with an upper and lower part (respectively the tergum and sternum). These are joined on each side by a flexible fold that allows the abdomen to expand and contract, providing an aid to breathing. The abdomen has relatively few appendages – it usually supports just the external sex organs and, in some of the more primitive insects, two tails (cerci) at the tip, which are sometimes accompanied by a third central one. Females may have a conspicuous egg-laying organ (ovipositor) at the end of the abdomen.

Unlike vertebrates, insects do not hear through ears on the head. The 'ears' are situated on various parts of the body – the legs, abdomen and even the wings – according to the type of insect. Insect ears are usually designed for detecting just those sounds produced by others of their own species, and the audible frequency range is thus rather limited.

This grasshopper's 'ear' is on the first segment of its abdomen.

# INSIDE THE BODY

Insects differ markedly from vertebrates in the way they breathe and excrete, in the circulation of their blood, and in the arrangement of the nervous system.

## Respiration

Insects have no lungs, and they do not actively breathe. Air enters the body through small apertures (spiracles) situated along the sides of the body. The spiracles, which can be opened or closed to control loss of moisture, are connected to a system of fine tubes (tracheae and tracheoles). These carry air to all parts of the body, and are sometimes helped by rhythmical contractions and expansions of the abdomen. The arrangement works very well over short distances, but becomes increasingly inefficient as the length of the tubes increases with the size of the insect. The maximum size of an insect is therefore limited by its breathing system.

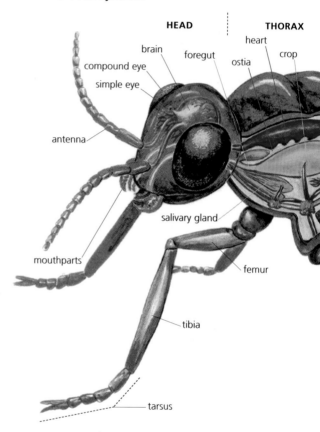

HEAD — THORAX

brain, foregut, heart, ostia, crop, compound eye, simple eye, antenna, salivary gland, mouthparts, femur, tibia, tarsus

## Circulation

Instead of blood vessels, insects have a blood-filled cavity (haemocoel) that occupies most of the body. All the internal organs lie in this cavity, and are bathed in the blood (haemolymph). A simple tubular heart in the thorax and abdomen runs along the back and pumps the blood forwards through the aorta in the thorax and into the head. From here the blood passes backwards in the haemocoel to circulate around the body before re-entering the heart through special valves (ostia). Again, unlike vertebrates, the blood has no respiratory function: its main purpose is to circulate nutrients and waste products and to distribute hormones to their appropriate sites. Moreover, it carries special cells that combat disease or help heal wounds, and is used to increase internal pressure in certain organs – for instance, when a newly emerged adult's wings expand. It may also be released from the joints as a defence against predators.

## Reproduction and excretion

Salts and nitrogenous waste matter pass through the Malpighian tubules, between the mid- and hindgut. The tubules serve much the same purpose as a mammal's kidneys. The reproductory organs are also indicated in green.

## Nervous system

This is well developed. In each segment of the body there is a ventral pair of nerve centres with nerves connecting with the insect's muscles and sense organs. The nerve centres are linked together by a nerve cord which runs the length of the body and joins up with the brain. The main purpose of the brain is to initiate reaction in response to information received from the antennae and eyes.

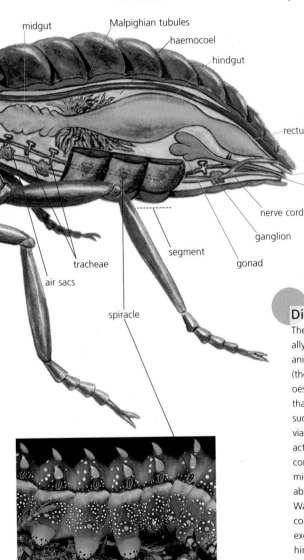

**ABDOMEN**

midgut
Malpighian tubules
haemocoel
hindgut
rectum
anus
genitalia
nerve cord
ganglion
segment
gonad
tracheae
air sacs
spiracle

Insects breathe through their spiracles.

## Digestive system

The way insects digest their food is basically the same as that of most other animals. The foregut starts with a pharynx (the canal between the mouth and the oesophagus) which, especially in insects that have liquid diets, acts as a pump to suck up the fluid. From here, food passes via the oesophagus into the crop, which acts as a temporary reservoir. The gizzard controls the passage of the food into the midgut. Most of the digestion and nutrient absorption processes occur in the midgut. Water is extracted by the hindgut to concentrate the solid waste, ready for excretion. At the junction of the mid- and hindgut are found the so-called Malpighian tubules (see Reproduction and excretion, above).

# INSECT GROUPS

Insects are one of several classes that make up the phylum Arthropoda. They are classified into various categories as shown in the list (below right) featuring the robber fly.

There are 26 orders of insects in all, divided into two subclasses. The first one, the Apterygota, includes all the primitive wingless insects that go through little or no metamorphosis (physical change from young to adult). Apterygota consists of just two orders.

The second subclass, Pterygota, contains all the winged insects together with those whose ancestors had wings but have since lost the power of flight. The Pterygota show varying degrees of metamorphosis during their growth, so we have broken the subclass down into two groups: first, those with simple life cycles (Exopterygota, which means 'external wings') in which the young develop gradually, the nymphs looking more or less the same as their parents; and second, those with complex life cycles (Endopterygota, or 'internal wings'). Insects in the latter group go through distinct larval and pupal stages during which they are quite unlike the adults in appearance.

Below each heading we give the name of the order and the number of its species known to occur in southern Africa. In most cases these are estimates only: many species have yet to be properly documented; others almost certainly await discovery. Altogether, we feature 19 of the 26 insect orders; those omitted are the inconspic-uous web-spinners (Embioptera), the booklice and psocids (Psocoptera), the stoneflies (Plecoptera), the alderflies (Megaloptera), the scorpion flies (Mecoptera), the thrips (Thysanoptera), and an exclusively African group of lice-like parasites (Hemimerina) that infest giant rats.

## THE SCHEME OF THINGS

Each living organism has its place in, and is defined by, a graded system of classification extending from the largest group (that is, either the animal or the plant kingdom) down the various levels to the specific name. For example, the robber fly *Lamyra gulo* fits in to the overall scheme as follows:

| | |
|---|---|
| Kingdom: | Animalia |
| Phylum: | Arthropoda |
| Class: | Insecta |
| Subclass: | Pterygota |
| Division: | Holometabola |
| | (or Endopterygota) |
| Order: | Diptera |
| Suborder: | Brachycera |
| Family: | Asilidae |
| Subfamily: | Laphriinae |
| Tribe: | Laphriini |
| Genus: | *Lamyra* |
| Species: | *gulo* |

**Left:** The typical cicada *Platypleura* sp., whose 'song' is a one of the more familiar sounds of Africa. **Above:** The strikingly patterned, flower-visiting beetle *Tragocephala formosa*.

# WINGLESS INSECTS
(Subclass Apterygota)

## Fishmoths
(Order Thysanura; 60 species)

These are well known for the damage they cause by eating paper, the glue in book bindings and other starch containing products. They have spindle-shaped bodies (which are slippery with a dense covering of scales), a pair of long thread-like antennae, and three long 'tails' at the tip of the abdomen. Many seldom-seen species live in leaf litter, some in the nests of ants and termites. Fishmoths are primitive insects, with a simple life cycle in which the young differ from their parents only in size, and are unusual in that they begin to breed before they are fully grown. They continue to moult throughout their lives, which can be as long as five years. Because of the second part of their common name ('moths') some people incorrectly believe them to be the young of clothes moths.

## Bristletails
(Order Archaeognatha; 19 species)

These insects are very similar to fishmoths in appearance, in their scaly bodies and life cycle. Unlike fishmoths, though, they have arched backs and, when disturbed, they can jump. None of them appears to be a pest of any kind.

Bristletails are more dependent on moisture than fishmoths and live on leaf litter, beneath bark, in rotting wood and under rocks. They eat algae, lichens, mosses and other moist vegetable matter. Some live permanently in ant and termite nests. They are commonly found in the indigenous forests of the eastern and southern Escarpment and coastal areas.

# INSECTS WITH SIMPLE LIFE CYCLES
(Subclass Pterygota; subdivision Exopterygota)

## Mayflies
(Order Ephemeroptera; 200 species)

Most adult mayflies live for only a few hours, hence the name of the order. They have two pairs of wings, the hind pair much smaller than the fore pair or even, sometimes, entirely absent. The wings are held together vertically over the body when the insect is at rest. The abdomen ends in either two or three long 'tails'. Males have elongated forelegs for holding females during mating flights.

These are delicate insects, often attracted by artificial lights and usually found near water – in which they lay their eggs, though some longer lived species keep these in their bodies for a while. The aquatic nymphs, or naiads, live on the beds of streams and pools and have gills along each side of the abdomen as well as the two, or three, 'tails'. They either feed on organic debris or are predatory, and may take two or three years to reach maturity, after which they emerge onto a twig or some other kind of support and almost immediately moult into a dull-coloured adult (known to fishermen as a 'dun'). Uniquely, the youngster soon moults again to become the perfect adult. Mayflies provide an important food source for fish, and so serve as models for many of the artificial lures used by anglers.

An adult mayfly. These fragile little insects are often attracted to artficial light.

# Dragonflies and Damselflies
(Order Odonata; 209 species)

Slender, often brightly coloured insects, frequently seen around rivers and dams. They have very large compound eyes and spiny, forward-placed legs that form a basket for scooping up prey on the wing. The four gauzy wings, all roughly the same size, move independently, allowing the insect to fly both forwards and backwards. Dragonflies and damselflies are easily told apart from the way they hold their wings at rest: the former horizontally to the side, or folded down and in front; the latter folded together over the abdomen or held half open. The young are aquatic predators, with the lower lip (labium) modified into a very efficient extendible organ, known as the mask, for grabbing insects, tadpoles and small fish.

A shield-like plate covers the cockroach's head; the end of the abdomen has two appendages.

abdomen, covering the delicate hindwings. Nymphs are small, wingless versions of their parents. All cockroaches are omnivorous.

These insects are only too well known to us, unpopular for the way some species invade and infest our homes. Among the latter are the large **American cockroach** and much smaller **German cockroach**. Many other types, however, live behind bark, in leaf litter or underneath stones and are not in any way troublesome. In fact they are seldom seen – except when attracted to artificial light. The large, tubby, wingless female of the endemic **mountain cockroach** (of the family Blaberidae) may occasionally be found under stones or crawling about in forest or fynbos in the southern and eastern Cape.

The dragonfly *Ictinogomphus ferox*, a species that defends its territory. The young are aquatic predators.

# Cockroaches
(Order Blattodea; 175 species)

Agile, flattened insects with a shield-like plate (pronotum) covering the head. They have long, thread-like antennae and two appendages (cerci) at the end of the abdomen. The winged species have leathery forewings that fold flat over the

A mountain cockroach *Aptera fusca* with her brood of nymphs.

# Termites
(Order Isoptera; 215 species).

Often but incorrectly called 'white ants', termites are not closely related to the true ants. But, like them, they are highly social creatures (see page 61). Each colony has soldiers, and workers that forage for food, care for the eggs and young and maintain the nest. The soldiers have large heads equipped with powerful mandibles for defence, or a special nozzle through which they squirt repellent or poisonous fluids at intruders. Unlike ants, though, the workers and soldiers are of both sexes, but sterile, and the colony has a resident king as well as the queen. A reproductive caste of winged males and females, known as alates, is periodically produced, leaving the nest in large flights to mate and establish new colonies. Females become egg-laying machines, and in some species their bodies become so distended that they can no longer move about. Kings remain with their queens to keep them fertilized.

**Dry-wood termites** (Kalotermitidae) and **damp-wood termites** (Rhinotermitidae) have the simplest nests, consisting merely of galleries in the dead branches of trees, in structural timber or, in the case of some members of the latter family, in the soil. **Harvester termites** (Hodotermitidae) forage in the open, cutting off pieces of vegetation, especially grass, which are then carried back to an underground nest. Well-pigmented bodies protect these insects from the sun.

Workers of the fungus-growers such as the *Macrotermes* (Termitidae) also forage in the open but are less well pigmented. Many of this family's members build nest mounds (termitaria; see pages 61–62); those that do not, such as *Odontotermes*, make earthen runways on the stems of plants.

Several species are serious pests, attacking structural timber, furniture, crops and pasture grasses. However, many others are beneficial, improving the aeration and moisture penetration of the soil, recycling plant material and bringing minerals to the surface. Except for the fungus-growers, all termite species carry, in their gut, micro-organisms that enable them to digest cellulose, the main constituent of plant cell walls.

# Praying Mantids
(Order Mantodea; 120 species)

With their ultra-mobile, triangular heads and large eyes, mantids are quite unmistakeable. Most species have wings that fold flat over the abdomen (the front pair are somewhat leathery). The common name derives from the stance taken up while they wait in ambush for prey: the forelegs, specially adapted for grasping an insect victim, are held together, folded, below and in front of the head as if in prayer. Forelegs are also used for self-defence, as are wings when spread out in a threat display. Thus armed, the larger mantids can deter birds and even a dog or cat.

The praying mantid's forelegs serve as efficient clamps for holding prey.

A termite queen, an egg-laying machine whose average life span is six to nine years.

## Earwigs
(Order Dermaptera; 52 species)

These long-bodied little creatures – they vary from 5 to 50 mm in length – carry a conspicuous pair of curved forceps at the end of the abdomen, which they use in courtship, self-defence and for holding prey. Winged species have large, ear-shaped hindwings that are folded away below the small, leathery forewings with the help of the forceps.

Earwigs are nocturnal, hiding by day below stones, in leaf litter, under bark, in sandy areas or in crevices. Almost half the 52 species found in southern Africa are endemic. *Forficula senegalensis* and *Labidura riparia* are widespread and typical, the latter commonly found on beaches.

Earwigs are among the relatively few insects that care for their young.

Praying mantids mating; the male may be eaten by his partner.

For the male, mating can be a hazardous business: he may well be eaten by his partner in the process! Eggs are laid in a foamy mass which hardens on drying, its shape varying according to the species but which is normally attached to plants and other objects. Some ground-living mantids place their egg cases in holes in the earth. Nymphs start fending for themselves straight after hatching and, characteristically, curl their abdomens over their backs.

Praying mantids are common and widespread; some endemic species occur in the arid southwest. Many species tend to be greenish, and are found among the foliage of trees and shrubs. Some conceal themselves on tree trunks, well disguised against the bark; a few live on the ground.

## Crickets, Grasshoppers and Katydids
(Order Orthoptera; estimated 820 species)

Most members of this very large order have long, strongly developed hindlegs which enable them to jump in spectacular fashion. Many are accomplished fliers as well. The leathery forewings fold back roof-wise over the abdomen, covering up the larger hindwings.

The long-horned species, those with antennae (or feelers) at least as long as the body and with a minimum of 30 segments, make up the suborder Ensifera. Those with antennae that are much shorter than the body, and with fewer than 30 segments, are the Caelifera.

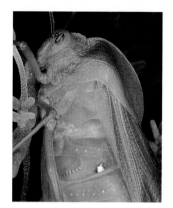

Left: The stridulating, or chirping, mechanism of a bladder grasshopper; the inflated abdomen acts as a sound box. Right: The Parktown prawn, *Libanasidus vittatus*, is a common and, to most people, repugnant presence in Gauteng gardens, but is quite harmless. Below: An armoured ground cricket.

The Ensifera are highly diverse, though females usually have long sword- or spear-shaped ovipositors (egg-laying appendages). Among them are wingless, ground-living species such as the only-too-familiar **Parktown prawn** (nocturnal insects that hide in burrows during the day), and the striking looking **armoured ground crickets**, which are active during the day. Then there are the well-camouflaged **katydids** that resemble leaves or lichen-covered bark. Males of many Ensifera species produce 'songs' by rubbing specially modified areas of the body together, a process known as stridulation (see page 45). The sounds are detected by 'ears' situated on the forelegs. Crickets are especially familiar to us because they come into our houses and burst forth, loudly, in chirruping song. Some also burrow into our lawns, often causing a great deal of damage. Mole crickets in fact feed on roots: their forelegs are wonderfully adapted for digging.

The Caelifera are the so-called short-horned grasshoppers. Some species have 'ears', which are located on the first abdominal segment. Most familiar are members of the family Acrididae, which are conspicuously active during the day and found just about everywhere, often in bewildering variety. Among family members are the **locusts** – several species of large grasshoppers that occur in solitary and gregarious 'phases'. The latter phase develops in response to overcrowd-

ing; populations then form into vast, voracious swarms that move across the countryside leaving a swathe of devastation in their wake. These pests must not, though, be confused with the brightly coloured (and therefore distasteful) **bush locusts** (family Pyrgomorphidae), whose nymphs form small swarms that usually disperse by the time they become adult. The family Pamphagidae contains the stone-like **toad grasshoppers** and some especially large species (the females of many of these are wingless). The males of the well-named **bladder grasshoppers** (Pneumoridae) have inflated abdomens which act as sound resonators: the insects generate weird night-time calls by rubbing special ridges on the side of the abdomen with their hindlegs.

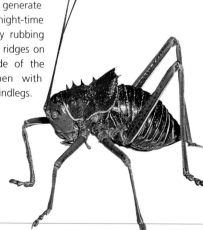

## Stick Insects
(Order Phasmatodea; 50 species)

This large stick insect, *Palophus reyi*, is camouflaged to perfection.

These elongated insects are masters of disguise, maintaining an uncanny resemblance to twigs or grass stems. Surprisingly, despite their rather cumbersome shape, some species are able to fly. The forewings are short, leathery and do not fully cover the tightly folded hindwings which, when the occasion demands, are suddenly flashed open to frighten away an intruder.

All stick insects are vegetarian, and lay their eggs on the ground – in some cases the eggs are equipped with a removable appendage called a capitulum by which foraging ants carry the egg back to their nest. The ants eat the capitulum but the egg remains unharmed – a process which helps both to disperse and to protect the eggs (especially from fire). Nymphs are surprisingly resilient and well adapted for survival: if grasped by a predator they will simply discard the limb and grow a new one.

## Lice
(Order Phthiraptera; 1 100 species)

These are flattened, wingless insects (though their ancestors had wings) adapted for living on mammals and birds as external parasites. **Sucking lice** (Anoplura) extract the host's blood through piercing mouthparts and occur only on mammals (their legs are specially adapted for clinging to hairs). The human louse, *Pediculus humanus*, occurs in two forms: the **head louse**, which attaches its eggs to the hair; and the **body louse**, which lives generally on the body, laying its eggs

on clothing. The crab louse *Phthirus pubis*, another species that parasitizes humans, also glues its eggs to hairs.

**Feather** and **biting lice** (Mallophaga), which live on birds and mammals, have chewing

A feather louse

mouthparts which they use to feed on feathers, hair, skin fragments and blood from wounds. These tiny creatures are adept at moving about their hosts through fur or feather.

## Bugs
(Order Hemiptera; 4 000 species)

A huge and diverse order which includes many pest species. All its members have piercing and sucking mouthparts; many feed on plant juices, some on the body fluids of other insects or on blood. Only a few can be mentioned here.

It is plain to see how shield bugs acquired their name; this is a common member of the family.

Bugs of the suborder Heteroptera (meaning 'different wings') have leathery forewings with membranous outer parts that are folded over the abdomen. One subdivision comprises the 'water bugs', among which are those giant members of the family Belostomatidae, fearsome predators that reach 70 mm in length and happily attack fish, tadpoles, frogs and fellow insects. Other aquatic members of the subdivision include the **water scorpions** (Nepidae), which are also predatory, and recognizable by the long breathing tube or siphon at the end of the abdomen;

The assassin bug *Ectrichodia crux* is an accomplished flier. The Hemiptera is among the largest of orders.

*Paropioxys jucundus* is one of the bigger and more beautiful of the plant hoppers.

the much smaller, carnivorous **backswimmers** (Notonectidae), and the mostly vegetarian **waterboatmen** (Corixidae). **Pond skaters** (Gerridae) live on the water, supported by the surface tension, scavenging on dead insects. Water bugs can often be seen in domestic swimming pools.

The rest of the insects in the suborder are land-living. **Shield bugs** (Pentatomidae), also known as 'stink bugs', are for the most part sapsuckers (though a few do hunt for prey) that give off pungent smells when disturbed. They glue batches of eggs to leaf surfaces, and the newly hatched nymphs may encircle the empty shells for a while before dispersing. **Tip wilters** (Coreidae) feed at the bases of flower buds and shoots, causing them to wilt. Some species squirt a spray of smelly fluid from the anus if attacked. The brightly coloured nymphs and adults of **cotton stainers** (Pyrrhocoridae) often gather on bolls of cotton and related plants to feed on the seeds. The predatory **assassin bugs** (Reduviidae) have strong, curved probosces and can deliver painful bites; the species *Ectrichodia crux* feeds on millipedes, on which clusters of the bright red nymphs can often be seen.

By contrast with the Heteroptera, bugs in the suborder Homoptera (meaning 'similar wings') have uniformly membranous forewings that fold roof-wise over the abdomen. All are plant feeders. The familiar **cicadas** (Cicadidae), incorrectly called Christmas bees or beetles, are best known for the shrill, rasping calls produced by the males. Their nymphs feed below ground on root sap and, when mature, emerge to climb up the nearest plant, where the adult emerges. You can often see the empty nymphal skins on the branches and trunks of trees. **Leaf hoppers**

Most of the assassin bugs are predators of other insects, which they pierce with their beaks.

These bright red nymphs of the predator *Ectrichodia crux* are feeding on a millipede.

(family Cicadellidae), on the other hand, are mostly small, inconspicuous insects, but for all their modesty include several serious pests in their ranks, one of which (*Cicadulina mbila*) is the vector of maize streak virus. Nymphs of the **spittlebugs** (Cercopidae) cover themselves with a froth, known as 'cuckoo spit' – made by bubbling a fluid from the anus (see page 54) – a novel defence against predators. Members of one species, *Ptyelus grossus*, are known as **'rain tree bugs'** because they produce so much of the fluid that it falls to the ground like a continuous, gentle downpour.

There are several families of **plant hoppers**, among them some very attractive, moth-like insects such as species of *Paropioxys*. *Melicharia* bugs are sometimes seen in rows on stems of shrubs, aggregations that are carried to extremes in the family Flatidae: adult groupings of some species look for all the world like inflorescences. Species of *Pyrops* have greatly elongated heads that make them look like broken twigs.

Many of the species of **aphid** or **greenfly** (Aphididae) are only too well known to gardeners and farmers, forming dense, damaging clusters on young shoots and leaves. They expel their excess liquids and sugars through the anus, thus attracting ants. The ants protect and even 'farm' the aphids in much the same manner in which scale insects are nurtured (see below). Aphid numbers rapidly build up, partly due to this curious symbiotic relationship and partly because the females are able to give birth to live nymphs without having to mate.

Adults of the **scale insects** and **mealy bugs** (Coccidae and related families) are not readily recognizable as insects at all. Females are sedentary and degenerate, their bodies covered by wax threads, a thickened cuticle or a hard scale made from previously cast nymphal skins. Eggs and young are protected under the parent scales. Some – the red scale insect, for example – are serious citrus and other crop pests. Soft scales (Coccidae) produce honeydew which, like the aphid secretions (see above), attracts ants that tend the scales and drive off parasites, encouraging the spread of the infestation.

# INSECTS WITH COMPLEX LIFE CYCLES
(Subclass Pterygota; subdivision Endopterygota)

## Lacewings and Antlions
(Order Neuroptera; 350 species)

Members of this order have two pairs of large, similar-sized, membranous wings which, together with a long abdomen, makes some of the antlions look at first glance like dragonflies. However, in contrast to those of the dragonflies, the wings are usually folded roof-wise over the body.

Owlfly larvae hunt their prey on the branches of trees and bushes or among leaf litter.

Adults and larvae of most species are predatory, the larvae equipped with large sickle-shaped mouthparts for holding the prey and sucking out the liquid contents. **Thread-wing lacewings** (Nemopteridae) and some **green lacewings** (Chrysopidae) feed on pollen and nectar. The latter are delicate insects that seldom exceed 25 mm in length and whose eggs, uniquely, are attached to long stalks, probably as a defence against predators. Larvae and adults feed on aphids and scale insects, to the benefit of farmers and gardeners.

Like those of the praying mantids, the forelegs of adult **mantidflies** (Mantispidae) are designed for seizing prey. Their larvae feed on young cocooned spiders as they hatch from their eggs.

The adult forms of some of the **antlions** (Myrmeleontidae) are large and showy. Larvae live freely in sand, a few species catching prey in the familiar conical pitfall traps.

**Owlflies** (Ascalaphidae) have very long, clubbed antennae from which the insects' alternative name, **long-horned antlions**, derives. Their well-camouflaged larvae live on the trunks and branches of trees or among stones and leaves.

# Beetles
(Order Coleoptera; 18 000 species)

The largest order in the entire animal kingdom, found in all shapes, sizes and colours and in almost every conceivable environment. All its members, however, have biting mouthparts, and their forewings are characteristically modified as hardened cases (elytra) which protect the hindwings and which, when closed, fit tightly together (in flightless species, they may be fused). A tough cuticle also provides protection from physical damage. Many of the plant-feeders are pests. Here we mention just a few of the more important families.

The distinctive markings of this swift-running ground beetle warn of its ability to spray acid.

**CARABOID BEETLES** This distinctive group includes the swift-moving, ground-living **tiger beetles** (Cicindellidae), the **ground beetles** (Carabidae) and the aquatic **water beetles** (Dytiscidae) and **whirligig beetles** (Gyrinidae). All are predatory, as both larvae and adults. Except for some striking species of the genus *Mantichora*, tiger beetles take readily to the wing. Ground beetles have no wings and many, among them *Anthia* and *Thermophilum*, often sport warning colours advertising their chemical defences. Water beetles are commonly encountered when they fly into lights at night; whirligigs glide about on the surface of water, mostly in groups, but readily dive when alarmed.

Dung beetles show admirable perseverence in rolling their balls of dung to suitable burial sites.

**SCARABAEOID BEETLES** These are robust, mostly black or brown insects, most familiar of them perhaps the **dung beetles** (Scarabaeinae) – especially those that roll balls of dung away to the security of a burrow either to eat or to make into brood balls for the eggs. Other dung beetles, such as the large *Heliocopris* and the much smaller *Proagoderus* species, burrow directly below dung pads. Still others make their brood balls within the dung pad itself. With the exception of a few, including the flightless Addo dung beetle, most are active fliers.

Rather similar are the **rhinoceros beetles** (Dynastinae) whose young are the familiar white grubs that feed in manure and compost heaps. The males of some of the larger species are distinguished by a prominent, curved horn on the head.

**Fruit chafers** (Cetoniinae) feed on nectar, fruit and flowers, or on fermenting sap exuded from trees; the smaller chafers of the subfamily Rutelinae, many of which are nocturnal, live on foliage and flowers and can cause a great deal of damage – as do their C-shaped white grubs, which eat plant roots.

**BUPRESTOID BEETLES** The day-flying **jewel beetles** (Buprestidae), named for their strikingly brilliant metallic colouring and the sole members of the superfamily Buprestoidea, are characteristically wedge-shaped and have an extraordinarily hard cuticle. Some species reach 50 mm and more in length, and may have their bodies covered with brightly coloured tufts of wax-coated setae or hairs. Some visit flowers for the pollen. Their larvae feed in plant stems.

**ELATEROID BEETLES** These are the **click beetles** (family Elateridae), best known for their ability to right themselves when stranded on their backs, in the process making loud clicking sounds (see page 70). Click beetle larvae are known as 'wireworms' and live in compost, decaying wood or in the soil.

A typical click beetle of the family Elateridae.

The jewel beetle *Julodis hirsuta* in its coat of colourful wax tufts.

**Cantharoid beetles** Best known in this group are the **glow-worms** and **fireflies** (Lampyridae), whose adults signal with 'cold' light to attract a mate (see page 44). Another common family is that of the **netwinged beetles** (Lycidae), conspicuous black-and-orange insects, often with expanded forewings, that congregate on flowers and other herbage. All larval stages of cantharoid beetles are predatory; adults of most species are distasteful to other predators.

**Above:** A netwinged beetle in its warning colours. These insects can be seen congregating on flowers.
**Below:** Most ladybirds are welcome garden insects: they feed on aphids and other pests.

**Bostrychoid beetles** The damage caused by these insects is perhaps more familiar to the average person than the perpetrators themselves. Larvae of **death watch beetles** (Anobiidae), for example, attack stored foodstuffs, seasoned timber and furniture; **powder post beetles** (Lyctidae) feed on freshly cut and seasoned timber. All of them leave tell-tale 'worm holes'.

**Cucujoid beetles** Both the adults and larvae of most **ladybird beetles** (Coccinellidae) feed on aphids and scale insects and are therefore beneficial, though those in the subfamily Epilachninae are vegetarians. With their characteristic

shapes and red-and-black warning coloration, ladybirds are easily recognizable. The plant feeders are duller in colour than the predators.

Among the **darkling beetles** (Tenebrionidae) is a variety of flightless, ground-dwelling insects, including several desert-adapted species (see page 11) and the familiar **tok-tokkies**. Adults and their subterranean larvae feed on plant material and dead insects. Quite different from these are the species of *Tribolium* that infest flour, and the yellow mealworm *Tenebrio molitor*, whose larvae are often reared as food for cage birds.

**Blister beetles** (Meloidae), known locally as C.M.R. beetles (after the black-and-yellow banded uniform of the old Cape Mounted Rifles), expel distasteful fluid if handled; their soft bodies contain the poison cantharadin. Adults congregate on flowers to feed and mate. The larvae, hatching from eggs laid in the soil, search for the egg pods of grasshoppers and, if successful, will moult into fat inactive grubs. The larvae of some species, though, lie in wait on flowers, attach themselves to visiting bees and, once in the nest, feed on the host's larvae.

A blister beetle; all insects have a pair of sensory antennae, or 'feelers', on the head.

**Chrysomeloid beetles** Most striking of these are the **longicorn beetles** (Cerambycidae), all of which have very long antennae. Numerous brightly coloured day-flying species visit flowers, many mimicking distasteful or dangerous insects. Larvae of all species feed in either wood or the stems of herbaceous plants. The very varied and abundant **leaf beetles** (Chrysomelidae) feed on plant foliage; probably the most noticeable are the **tortoise beetles** (Cassidinae), among them the rather beautiful, metallic gold-coloured

A colourful day-flying longicorn beetle. The family includes some of the largest of insects.

*Aspidomorpha tecta*. The spiny larvae of the tortoise beetles cover themselves with their caste skins and excrement for camouflage.

**CURCULIONOID BEETLES** The heads of these insects are extended into an elongate snout, with the mouthparts at the tip. Both the adults and larvae are plant feeders. The largest family, the **weevils** (Curculionidae), includes those pests which feed on stored grain and crops such as maize (these are known as **snout beetles**). Many, however, occur on plants, among them some surprisingly bright-coloured species. The **lily weevils** (Brachycerinae), often found on the ground, include some of the largest curculionoid species. When touched, lily weevils will sham death.

The broad-nosed lily weevil *Brachycerus ornatus* playing dead in self-defence.

# Flies
## (Order Diptera; 6 260 species)

Insects in this huge group have only one pair of wings, the hind pair reduced to small club-shaped structures called halteres (see page 18) which help maintain balance in flight. All flies feed on liquids – nectar, the body fluids of other insects, blood from vertebrate animals – and their mouthparts are adapted accordingly. Blood feeders transmit serious diseases such as malaria, sleeping sickness and elephantiasis. Most species lay eggs, a few produce live young. All larvae are legless maggots, though there is enormous diversity in maggot feeding habits between the various species.

Only a few representative families can be mentioned here. There are three suborders.

**NEMATOCERA** The most primitive suborder, this consists mostly of slender, delicate flies with very long, fragile legs. **Crane flies** (Tipulidae) are the familiar 'daddy-long-legs' which look like enormous mosquitoes and which you often see in your home. Adults are either nectar feeders or do not feed at all; their tough-skinned larvae are either predatory or vegetarian. **Mosquitoes** themselves (Culicidae) are much smaller. Adults of both sexes are also nectar feeders, but the females (the carriers of disease) also suck blood from vertebrate hosts. Eggs are laid in water and either float in rafts or sink to the bottom. Larvae (commonly known as 'wrigglers') and pupae are aquatic, the latter unusual in their ability to swim about, though they do not feed.

Crane flies are usually found near water, in rank vegetation. Some species are attracted to light.

**BRACHYCERA** This suborder comprises robust, strong-flying flies of varying habits. **Horseflies** (Tabanidae) have large, often iridescently coloured eyes and are well known for the persistent though silent attacks and painful bites of the blood-sucking females. Males feed mostly on nectar. Larvae are predatory, living either in damp soil or beneath stones at water's edge. Several of the smaller *Haematopota* species have mottled wings and are sometimes called 'clegs'; some of them are bee-like and habitually rest on tree trunks.

**Robber flies** (Asilidae) catch insects in flight from a perch, grabbing them with their strong, bristly legs and sucking them dry. Some mimic certain wasps and bees. Larvae are either scavengers, vegetarian or predatory, and live in burrows in the soil or in rotting wood.

**Bee flies** (Bombyliidae) are mostly plump, hairy, bee-like insects with long probosces, projecting permanently in front, for sucking nectar from flowers. Some species hover above bare ground to drop their eggs into the open burrows of bees and wasps. Young larvae search for grasshopper eggs or the immatures of other insects and then moult into inactive grubs.

Adult **soldier flies** (Stratiomyiidae) are often brightly coloured or wasp-like insects that frequent flowers or over-ripe fruit. At rest, their wings fold scissor-wise over the abdomen. Larvae vary greatly; some are scavengers of decaying vegetation (for example in compost heaps), others aquatic and predatory.

Among the most spectacular looking members of this suborder are the **tangle-veined flies** (Nemestrinidae), some of which have extraordinarily long probosces that fold away underneath during flight.

**CYCLORRHAPHA** This suborder contains the more advanced species, those more generally recognized as flies. One subdivision, Aschiza, encompasses the well-known **hoverflies** (Syrphidae), which are often brightly coloured and hover over flowers. Many resemble bees and wasps. Larvae of some species feed on aphids, others on decaying vegetable matter. The 'rat-tailed maggots' are aquatic species – you'll often find them in livestock drinking troughs – that are equipped with long breathing tubes.

Another subdivision, Acalyptratae, contains a confusing array of families and species, among them the **fruit flies** (Tephritidae). Many are serious pests: eggs are inserted into the fruit, which is ultimately destroyed by the larvae that, when mature, drop to the ground to pupate. Adults, often attracted to fermenting liquids, have characteristically marbled wings, with the tip of the abdomen drawn out into a rigid ovipositor.

**Above left:** The robber fly *Proagonistes praeceps*.
**Above:** A blowfly of the genus *Lucilia*. Adults feed, with specially adapted mouthparts, on rotten meat and excrement.

Flies in the third subdivision, Calyptratae, form a more uniform group of 'typical' and very well-known families. These include the **houseflies** (Muscidae), the metallic green or blue **blowflies** and **bluebottles** (Calliphoridae) and the **fleshflies** (Sarcophagidae). Adults congregate on carrion, exposed meat and excrement, mopping up food with specially modified mouthparts. The saliva discharged to dissolve some foods can transmit diseases, such as typhoid and dysentery, previously picked up while feeding on contaminated waste. Larvae of houseflies develop in decaying organic matter. Blowfly larvae, often present in huge numbers, develop in carrion and excrement. Some blowflies and fleshflies parasitize the nests of wasps and bees.

Included in this subdivision are the well-known **tsetse flies** (Glossinidae), blood-sucking insects that transmit sleeping sickness in humans and nagana in livestock. They are distinctive, brownish creatures with a proboscis projecting in front of the head. The wings fold scissor-like over the abdomen.

**Tachinid flies** (Tachinidae) frequent flowers to feed on the nectar. Many resemble fleshflies; some are especially bristly; all are internal parasites of other insects: females attach their eggs to the bodies of their hosts, or to leaves to be swallowed by another insect. The mature maggots leave what remains of their hosts to pupate nearby.

## Fleas
(Order Siphonaptera; 98 species)

These are blood-sucking external parasites of birds and mammals, flattened laterally and highly resistant to being squashed. They do not have wings, but are excellent jumpers. Unlike lice (see page 29), their eggs simply fall to the ground, usually into the host's resting place. Larvae feed on organic debris, and especially on dried blood particles voided by the adult fleas.

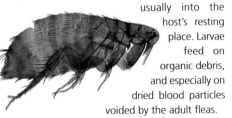

## Caddisflies
(Order Trichoptera; over 200 species)

Caddisflies are moth-like insects, distinguishable from moths by their clothing of hairs instead of overlapping scales. Most are scavengers. The larvae are aquatic, and many species make portable cases in which to live. Fully grown larvae anchor their cases and pupate inside, the pupa finally chewing its way out to crawl up to the surface, where the adult emerges.

The hairy covering to the wings of caddisflies distinguishes them from similar looking moths.

## Butterflies and Moths
(Order Lepidoptera; about 10 000 species)

These are undoubtedly the most 'popular' insects, mainly because of their grace and beauty. The order's name derives from the tiny overlapping scales which cover their wings ('lepis' means scale, 'pteron' means wing).

The most commonly asked question is: 'What's the difference between a butterfly and a moth?', and the simple answer is that there is no really clear scientific distinction. However, butterflies are usually brightly coloured, fly by day, fold their wings vertically above the body when at rest, and have clubbed antennae. Moths on the other hand are usually nocturnal and often sombrely coloured, though there are some brightly hued day fliers and not a few beautifully marked nocturnal species, among them the **emperor moths** (Saturniidae) and **hawk moths** (Sphingidae). At rest, moths fold their wings roof-wise over or wrapped around the body or laid flat against the substrate. They have various kinds of antennae, sometimes feathery, but never clubbed.

A gold-banded forester butterfly adds a splash of colour to the gloomy forest floor.

The sudden flash of this emperor moth's 'eyes', on its hindwings, can deter a predator.

Most adult butterflies and moths have long, tubular probosces for sucking up liquids such as nectar, fermenting tree sap or juices from over-ripe fruit. When the insects are not feeding, their probosces remain coiled up like watch-springs. In the fruit-piercing moths the proboscis is modified for breaking the skin of fruit. One species of the genus *Arcyophora* uses its proboscis for drinking the eye fluids of large mammals.

All butterflies and moths lay eggs, singly or in clumps, usually attaching them to the appropriate food plant. On hatching, the larvae, which are known as caterpillars, often eat their eggshells.

Caterpillars have well-developed heads with strong chewing mandibles, and there are three pairs of single-clawed legs on the segments of the thorax and two to five pairs of fleshy false legs (prolegs) on the abdomen. Otherwise the variations are endless: caterpillars can be smooth (Sphingidae, Geometridae, Noctuidae), densely covered in long hairs (Arctiidae), have various types of spines (Saturniidae) including those that

sting (Limacodidae) or regular tufts of hairs like the bristles on a toothbrush (Lymantriidae). Others resemble twigs (Geometridae) or are rarely seen because they burrow into wood (Cossidae). Bagworms (Psychidae) make portable cases out of sticks or leaves. Caterpillars of some species of blues (Lycaenidae) spend most of their lives living in ants' nests, where they are cared for in return for sweet secretions from special glands.

Before reaching the adult stage, fully grown caterpillars change into pupae. Butterfly pupae are naked and attached to their food plant or some other support. Moth pupae are usually enclosed in a silken cocoon.

The caterpillars of many species are serious pests, among them the army worm, maize stalk borer, red bollworm, golden plusia, cutworms, American bollworm, pine tree emperor, fruit-piercing moth, Angoumois grain moth and clothes moth. Some, however, are actually used to control plant invaders (the prickly pear moth is an example).

## Wasps, Bees and Ants
(Order Hymenoptera; well over 6 000 species).

This order contains more species that bring benefit to man than any other. The behavioural patterns of many of its members are remarkably advanced; some wasps and bees and all ants have evolved a highly developed social life.

Most bees and many wasps lay their eggs in prepared nests. The adults feed on nectar. The bees and a few wasps feed their young with nectar and pollen; all other wasps – except for sawflies, which belong to a different suborder and whose offspring feed on foliage – provide

The young of butterflies and moths look quite different from their parents.

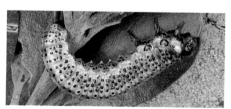

The caterpillar-like larva of the sawfly *Arge* sp., which eats plant matter. Adults feed at flowers.

their offering with paralysed insects or spiders, or are parasitic on other insects.

The adults of the order have two pairs of membranous wings (the hind pair are the smaller) and biting mouthparts. The latter, though, are often modified for sucking and lapping liquids as well. There is usually a waist between the thorax and abdomen. Females of most species have well-developed ovipositors, but some use these for stinging in self-defence or for paralysing prey.

The most primitive members of the order are the **sawflies** (suborder Symphyta), which are usually waistless and, for the most part, yellow insects. Here the ovipositor is modified as a saw for cutting slits in plants, into which they deposit their eggs. Sawfly larvae, which look much like the caterpillars of butterflies and moths, feed on plants; the adults feed at flowers.

All other members of the order Hymenoptera fall into the suborder Apocrita, which has two divisions: the Parasitica and Aculeata. The latter contains all the ants and the more familiar wasps and bees.

**WASPS** The division Parasitica contains legions of often minute species that lay their eggs in the eggs or larvae of other insects, and thus play a valuable role in regulating their hosts' numbers. Their larvae develop within the bodies of their hosts and are called 'internal parasitoids'. The small, silky cocoons you sometimes see attached to caterpillars are spun by the parasitic larvae that have emerged from their hosts to pupate. More conspicuous species occur among the **ichneumon flies** (Ichneumonidae) such as *Osprynchotus* (see page 77). Those bright red or orange wasps that one glimpses flying about vegetation or resting on branches are likely to be **braconids** (Braconidae), which often have very long ovipositors designed for tunnelling into plant stems, where they lay eggs in the larvae of wood-boring moths and beetles.

Certain families in the division Aculeata are also parasitic. In some of them the larvae feed externally on the bodies of their hosts, and are called 'external parasitoids'. **Scoliids** (Scoliidae), for instance, are heavy-looking, bristly wasps that frequent manure and compost heaps intent on

**Above:** A pollen wasp at the turreted entrance to its nest. Some species build their nests in the ground, others on plants or stones. **Top:** The striking patterns of this velvet ant warn of its painful sting.

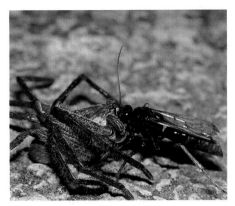

A spider-hunting wasp with its prey, which it will defend with aggression.

parasitizing beetle larvae belonging to the family Scarabaeidae. The ant-like females of **velvet ants** (Mutillidae) are wingless, usually seen running about on the ground searching for the nests of ground-nesting bees and wasps, which many species parasitize. Some enter buildings in quest of mud dauber wasp nests. Others select immature stages of certain flies, beetles, moths and cockroaches as hosts. Their strident colours, mostly a combination of red, black and white, warn of the powerful sting they can deliver. The males are fully winged.

A few wasps and bees show a different type of parasitism. They lay their eggs on the prey of, or in the provisioned nest cells prepared by, other wasps and bees, and their larvae feed on the provision laid up by the host for its own young. These species are known as 'cleptoparasites'. Many species of **cuckoo wasps** (Chrysididae) are cleptoparasites: small, very active, bright metallic green insects whose larvae usually eat the host's larva as well as the provision.

The remainder of the wasp families consist mainly of free-living species, apart from some cleptoparasites among the spider-hunting wasps (Pompilidae) and solitary wasps (Sphecidae). The **spider-hunting wasps** are among the largest; some make a loud clicking noise with their wings when flying close to the ground; all hunt spiders, which they paralyse and drag into a prepared nest, burrow or pre-existing cavity. Having laid an egg on the victim, they seal and then abandon the nest. *Tachypompilus ignitus* is commonly seen dragging its paralysed rain spider victim towards its nest. A few species (subfamily Ceropalinae) are cleptoparasites of other spider-hunting wasps.

Similarly, **solitary wasps** make nests either in existing cavities or by digging burrows. A few build mud nests. The nests are stocked with paralysed insects or spiders, the type depending on the wasp species. Adult solitary wasps vary enormously in appearance, ranging from stocky, brightly coloured species of the *Stizus* and *Bembix* genera to sombre-coloured *Ammophila* with long, slender abdomens. Cleptoparasitic species occur in the subfamily Nyssoninae.

**Mason** and **potter wasps** (Eumenidae) make much more generous use of mud in preparing cells and building free mud nests. These range from the exquisitely made one-celled clay pots resembling Grecian urns to the massive, many-celled affairs constructed by *Synagris* mason wasps. The entrances to nests in the ground or in pre-existing cavities are often strikingly distinguished by mud turrets.

The only wasps to feed their young on pollen and nectar are the **pollen wasps** (Masaridae), solitary species that nest in mud-turreted burrows in the ground or mud cells that are attached to plants and stones.

**Paper wasps** (Vespidae) are social and use wood pulp to build their many-celled nests, which are attached to plants or, often, to buildings, and which are defended aggressively. These are brownish, often long-waisted insects that feed their larvae directly with chewed caterpillars.

**BEES** All bees belong to the superfamily Apoidea, and those that are solitary have much in common in their behaviour with solitary wasps, though all provision their nests with pollen and nectar. There are several families, within each of which there is great diversity. Most, however, include species that nest in pre-existing or self-made burrows.

**Carpenter bees** (Xylocopinae), of the family Anthophoridae, drill large burrows in wood, including roof beams and fence posts. The family Megachilidae contains the **leaf cutters** (*Megachile*), notable for the way they use cut

The entrance to a nest of stingless bees is guarded by workers.

pieces of leaves for making and partitioning their nests. In contrast, *Chalicodoma* and *Hoplitis* species use resin, mud and pebbles for the same purpose. The **sweat bees** (Halictidae) comprise a range of solitary to social species. All three families include cleptoparasitic species.

All species of the family Apidae are social (see page 65), the most familiar of them perhaps the **honeybee** *Apis mellifera* and the stingless **mopane bees** *Trigona* The latter are well known for the way they try to obtain moisture from peoples' eyes and mouths.

**ANTS** These belong to the very large family Formicidae and are the most advanced of all social insects (see page 67). Colonies range from the relatively small in the subfamily Ponerinae to the enormous in the subfamily Dorylinae. Many species nest in the ground, though the members of some subfamilies make nests in hollow twigs, reeds, thorns or, like the **cocktail** and **weaver ants**, in trees and bushes.

Each colony typically contains one queen and the wingless workers, some of which are soldiers. Except for those in the subfamilies Dolichoderinae and Formicinae, the workers have stings. Many species in these two subfamilies, and in the Myrmicinae, are pests because they 'farm' scale insects or aphids (see page 58); others, such as the **army ants** (Dorylinae) are carnivorous; the Cerapachyinae prey on other ants; the large species of the subfamily Ponerinae prey on termites. *Streblognathus aethiopicus*, which grows to fully 20 mm in length, is the largest of the southern African ants.

The ant *Paltothyreus tarsatus* lives on a specialized diet of termites.

*Streblognathus aethiopicus* lives in small colonies of just a few dozen members.

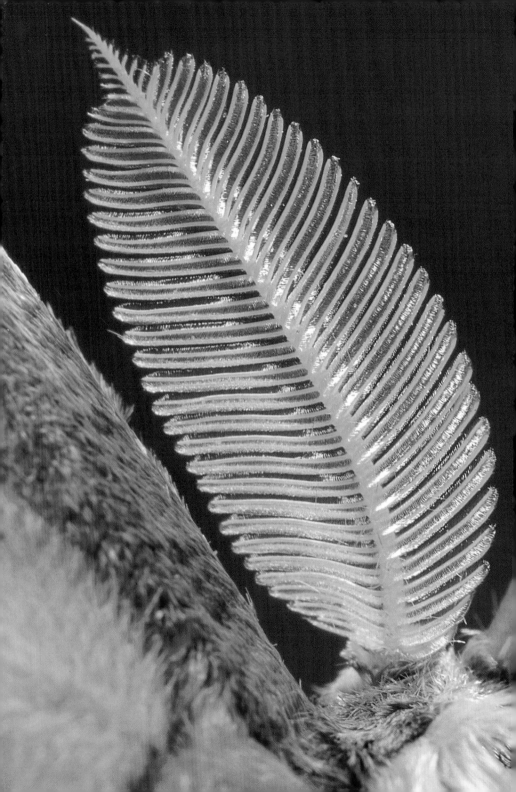

# FAMILY LIFE

Family life as we know it – that is, a male and female raising offspring and all living together – is uncommon in the insect world. One often sees gatherings of insects, but these are something else: in some instances the young of single females (some caterpillars, for example) staying together for feeding and protection, or adults joining up to sleep (certain wasps do this), eat or, in the case of various bugs and beetles, to over-winter. But none of these constitutes a real family.

Social species such as ants, bees and termites can of course be said to live in 'families' – in the sense that all the colony's inhabitants are the off-spring of just one resident female – but these teeming societies hardly fit our concept of the term, especially since the young are raised not by the parent but by the worker castes.

For the most part, female insects simply deposit their eggs in an appropriate place and then abandon them, though some species do go in for a degree of offspring care. Males seldom play any role at all in the rearing process, though here again there may be exceptions. A number of female water bugs, for instance, hi jack their part-ner into caring for the eggs, by simply attaching them to his back. The males of some assassin bugs play a slightly more active role, guarding the eggs and, for a few days after hatching, the young nymphs as well. Certain male dung beetles help pre-pare and provision the nest.

## Getting together

Finding a mate can be a daunting task, which insects tackle with the use of one or more of the senses: sight, hearing, smell – and, some of them, simply by eliminating competition.

**SIGHT** This is the simplest way to locate a partner, most dramatically exploited perhaps by those insects that form dancing aerial swarms. Male caddisflies, mayflies, midges and some dance flies all take to the air in numbers to lure females. Many other species, though, search in solitude. Some male butterflies are attracted by the move-ment, colour and shape of females; male digger wasps set out to look for females excavating bur-rows and then swoop on them. Others play the waiting game, congregating at sites, like water points, that are likely to be visited by females. The search is of course limited to daylight hours – except for the fireflies and glow-worms, which generate light signals (see box, page 44).

**Left:** The feathery antennae of many male moths are ultrasensitive to the scents (called pheromones) produced by the females. **Above:** Caterpillars of the species *Anaphe reticulata*. **Top right:** Male *Cerceris* wasps gather on a twig for the night.

# LIGHTS IN THE DARKNESS

Several forms of animal life produce their own light, but none do so more effectively than the beetles known as fireflies and glow-worms (family Lampyridae), essentially as signals to the opposite sex and aids to mutual species recognition. The luminosity may also act as a warning (of distastefulness) to predators.

The light is created in organs, located on the underside of the abdomen, that contain special photogenic cells backed by a layer of cells filled with white uric acid crystals (the layer acts as a reflector) and covered by a transparent window. The cells are richly endowed with nerves and air passages.

Light is created when a substance called luciferin is oxidized in the presence of water and an enzyme called luciferase. The oxygen necessary for the process arrives via the air passages. The firefly's intermittent flashes are controlled by the nerves.

This is the most efficient form of light production known to man: it is a cold luminosity (practically no heat is generated), and is confined to the visible spectrum – that is, it contains no infrared, ultraviolet or other invisible rays.

Female glow-worms are unique in the size, brilliance and complexity of their light-producing organs. They remain immobile, resting on vegetation, while they give out the steady glow that will attract a mate. By contrast, the male of the firefly takes to the air to emit bright pulses at species-specific frequencies. Females tend to be less active, responding with weaker pulses. Remarkably, though, some female fireflies mimic the flashing codes of other species to attract their males – which they then eat!

The steady light from a female glow-worm serves as a beacon for prospective partners.

**SOUND** The visual approach has its drawbacks – often, the more effective the display the more it will attract predators – and many species depend instead on sonic signals in their search for mates.

These insects do not always have a special apparatus for creating sound. The wing-beats of the female yellow-fever mosquito *Aedes aegypti*, for instance, produce its high-frequency whine; male tok-tokkies attract partners simply by tapping out a rhythm on the ground with the abdomen.

On the other hand male crickets, katydids and grasshoppers have developed specially modified parts of the body, which they rub together in order to produce their well-known chirping 'songs'; male cicadas, renowned for their piercing calls, have evolved incredibly elaborate organs at the base of the abdomen (see box, opposite).

This large tok-tokkie beetle, *Phanerotoma* sp., signals by tapping the ground.

# SOUNDS OF THE VELD

The masters of insect 'song' are undoubtedly the grasshoppers, katydids and crickets, which 'stridulate' by rubbing modified parts of the body together.

Crickets and katydids have a 'file', at the base of one of the forewings, which is rubbed by a thickened area (the 'scraper') at the edge of the other forewing. This generates wing vibrations, and hence the sound waves.

Perhaps the most characteristic sound of the hot African summer, though, is the shrill, almost ear-splitting call of the cicada. The noise, again, is produced only by the males, but in a quite different and far more complicated way. A covered ventral cavity on each side of the abdomen contains a drum-like, convex membrane called the tymbal. This is pulled in by a muscle, and pops out again

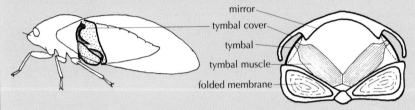

mirror
tymbal cover
tymbal
tymbal muscle
folded membrane

The location (left) and a cross section (right) of the cicada's stridulating or 'singing' mechanism.

In many acridid grasshoppers (Acrididae) either the front edge of the hindwing rubs against the lower surface of the forewing, or a thickened vein on the forewing is rubbed by the hind femur. But the most impressive calls are produced by male bladder grasshoppers (family Pneumoridae). These weird nocturnal sounds carry over long distances because they are amplified by the grossly inflated, air-filled abdomen. A row of pegs on each side of the abdomen forms the file over which the femur is scraped.

when the muscle relaxes, producing sound (at a frequency of up to 7 000 Hz) in much the same way as a curved tin lid will when pushed in. The cavity acts as a resonator, and the sound waves are amplified by other structures, inside the cavity, known as the 'folded membrane' and the 'mirror'. The cicada's call helps gather together all the males and females of a particular species into one fairly small area.

Many beetles – both male and female – also stridulate. Where exactly the sound-producing apparatus is located varies according to the species. For example, the ends of the wing covers of some scarab beetles and weevils are scraped over a file located on the top of the abdomen. In others, friction between the mouthparts, the first and second segments of the thorax or various parts of the legs create the vibrations.

And it seems that, in many cases, the sound has a lot more to do with self-defence than the mating process: many of the larger dung and longicorn beetles, for example, will stridulate when held against their will.

The blown-up abdomen of the male grasshopper *Pneumora inanis* serves as a sound resonator.

**Above:** Wasps of the family Tiphiidae are parasites of beetle larvae that live underground. **Below:** Mating welwitschia bugs. Many insects go through a courtship ritual that involves gifts or aphrodisiacs.

**Scents** Tantalizing aromas – from chemicals known as pheromones – are especially effective lures in the insect world, hugely extending the range of attraction. Many female moths have scent glands, at the end of the abdomen, which produce tiny quantities of pheromones that are picked up by the unbelievably sensitive, feathery antennae of the males at great distances. Female praying mantids and stick insects also give off inviting scents to declare their availability. The downside, though, is that pheromones can attract just too many males, resulting in a free-for-all, known as 'scramble competition', for access to the female.

**Excluding rivals** Competition can seriously reduce the chances of securing a partner, so some insects set up territories from which they aggressively exclude intruders. The males of many dragonfly and damselfly species patrol and defend their turf along streams or lake shores, mating with females who enter – and, in some insects, the enticement to do so is that much stronger if the male chooses a patch rich in flowers. Male carpenter bees deliberately select such areas.

## Bribery and seduction

Having found their partners, the two insects go through the courtship process, which often involves aphrodisiacs and nuptial gifts. The males of some cockroaches for instance exude a substance, presumed to contain a pheromone, from a gland on the abdomen, a secretion which the female touches or even eats, and which enhances her libido. Male butterflies such as the African monarch achieve the same result by exposing a potential mate's antennae to pheromones produced from brushes at the tip of the abdomen.

An alternative enticement is a nuptial gift in the form of food. The male scorpion fly, having caught his insect prey, uses scent to attract a female – who proceeds to eat the proffered meal while the male mates with her. In much the same way, male dance flies that carry gifts of prey in a mating swarm are first to be chosen by the females. Males of the genus *Hilara*, which usually wrap their gifts in silken balloons, sometimes cheat by carrying an empty package!

## The mating act

The seduction complete, the final mating phase can begin. This, in many insects, involves the insertion by the male of a sperm packet (spermatophore) into a special receptacle, the spermatheca, in the female's genital cavity. Often, part of the sperm packet is left protruding and this the female eats while the sperm is entering her reproductive system.

**SECURING THE INVESTMENT** The last sperm to be received by the female is the first to be used for fertilizing eggs – which makes sense: having gone to so much trouble to locate and mate with a partner, a male has to make sure that it is his sperm, and not that from a recent mating, that fertilizes the eggs. To this end, the males of a number of insects, including beetles, bugs, dragonflies and damselflies, guard their partners after mating and during egg-laying.

In fact the entire mating procedure in some dragonflies and damselflies is designed to ensure paternity. First, the male transfers sperm to a special receptacle below his second abdominal segment to free his abdomen. He then catches a female and holds her behind the head with special claspers at the tip of his abdomen, and for a while they fly about in tandem. When they finally settle, the female curls her abdomen, adopting

Some longicorn beetles ring-bark branches to provide dead wood for their larvae.

The 'wheel position' adopted by mating damselflies; the male is on the right.

the so-called 'wheel position' to bring the tip of her abdomen into contact with the male's receptacle, and to take up the sperm. Once copulation is complete, the pair again proceeds in tandem while the female lays her eggs. From start to finish, no other male has been allowed a look-in.

## Parental duties

**PROVIDING FOOD** The female's biggest investment in the future of the species is to make sure her young have enough to eat. Butterflies, moths and vegetarian bugs select the correct food plants and attach their eggs to the foliage or stems. Katydids cut slits, in which they deposit their eggs, in bark or leaves with their sword-like ovipositors. Longicorn

beetles insert their eggs into natural cracks in bark. Indeed some species go even further, ring-barking the branch so that it will die, the dead matter providing an ideal home for the larvae.

Parasitic wasps guarantee a food supply by finding a host and inserting the eggs into its body, some drilling into wood to reach the victim or, when the host is another wasp, through the mud walls of its nest. Some actually enter the host's nest to deposit their eggs. Parasitic flies stick their eggs directly onto the host's body or on their food (so that they are swallowed), or offload young larvae either on or near the host. The eggs of horse botflies are laid on a horse's forelegs, to be licked (when the animal grooms itself) and swallowed.

For predatory insects, the right environment is generally more important to the young's survival than finding a particular food item, though some do seek out prey, near which they lay their eggs. Ladybird beetles, hover flies and lacewings, for instance, deposit eggs close to or among the aphids on which they feed. Dragonfly and damselfly nymphs, on the other hand, hunt more mobile prey, so the airborne female simply drops her eggs in water, or, using her saw-like ovipositor, inserts them into the stems of water plants. Some predatory long-horned grasshoppers dig into the ground to lay their eggs and the nymphs, on hatching, find their way to the surface to begin hunting.

**CARING FOR THE EGGS** A rudimentary form of family life emerges when insects take parental care a step further, guarding the eggs until they hatch, and even guarding the young themselves. We have already seen that some female water bugs attach their eggs to the backs of their mates for safekeeping. The females of some cockroach species carry a hardened egg case protruding from the abdomen, later dropping it either before or at the time the eggs hatch. Thereafter the nymphs fend for themselves. Conversely, American cockroaches cover their egg cases with debris and glue them into a crevice. Some shield bugs and praying mantids simply stand guard over their eggs.

Alternatively, eggs may be kept inside the body until they hatch, in some instances even until the larvae are ready to pupate. Some flesh flies deposit young maggots in the nest entrances of ground-nesting wasps, the grubs then burrowing down to find their hosts. Tsetse flies have a quite different approach to rearing their young: the larvae are nourished one at a time within the abdomen, from a nipple connected to 'milk' glands. The larvae pupate almost immediately after being 'laid'.

This mountain cockroach *Aptera fusca* is brooding her family of newly born nymphs.

Tsetse flies are easily recognized by their forward-pointing probosces.

**BABY-SITTING** We have seen (page 43) that some dung beetles, assassin bugs and others continue to care for their young into the larval or nymphal stages. Other examples include the mountain cockroach, which gives birth to several live nymphs. These stay with their mother for several weeks, sheltering under her body or foraging for food nearby. Female earwigs lay their eggs in shallow burrows beneath stones and logs, caring for them, and for the young nymphs until they are able to fend for themselves. Mole and certain other crickets guard and care for their eggs in underground chambers, the entire family – the mother and her nymphs – emerging together after a few weeks in the chamber.

**MOTHERING THE YOUNG** Most solitary wasps and bees invest heavily in the protection of their young. They dig or make nests of varying complexity, stocking them with paralysed spiders or insects or with pollen and nectar. They then lay one egg in each nest cell, seal the nest and depart. Slightly more advanced are some species of *Ammophila* and *Bembix* wasps, which continue to bring in fresh food (paralysed caterpillars and flies respectively) for their developing larvae until they reach maturity. Even further advanced are the females of the genus *Synagris*, which remain in the cell, guarding the entrance while their larvae feed, and only leave to get fresh caterpillars for the larder. When one larva is fully grown the mother seals the cell and then starts on the next one.

In all these cases the mother alone provides the care. In a few others, the service is provided on a collective basis. Some spider-hunting wasps, for example, build mud cells in the hollow branches of trees or other cavities, and the hideaways are shared by several females, one of which acts as a guard. She will attack any unwelcome intruders such as parasitic wasps.

One of the mountain cockroach nymphs
(see opposite) in the act of moulting.

The mud-pot nest of the wasp *Afreumenes* sp.:
packed with paralysed caterpillars.

The ultimate in caring for the young is of course provided by the social insects: the termites, social wasps, social bees and ants. But this nurturing is no longer a family affair: the job is delegated, collectively, to the workers.

## Growth and change

One drawback of a rigid exoskeleton is that it prohibits the kind of regular, gradual growth enjoyed by vertebrates. An insect's outer covering, or cuticle, must therefore be changed at intervals, a process known as moulting or ecdysis.

Before each moult a new and larger cuticle is laid down beneath the old one. In this process much of the original material is dissolved and reabsorbed into the body, and the remaining outer layer splits along lines of weakness, usually on the head and thorax. The insect then drags itself out of its old cuticle and pumps itself up by swallowing air, so that the new cuticle is stretched to its maximum size before hardening. While moulting, the body is soft and delicate, especially vulnerable to injury and predation. Insects therefore often hide away, in well-sheltered spots, until their new skeletons have toughened and they can continue feeding.

Species moult several times (the average is five or six) before they reach the adult stage and, apart from an increase in size, may change dramatically not only in appearance but in habits as well. This striking process is known as metamorphosis (see also page 23).

As we've seen, the insect world can be divided into three broad groups according to the complexity of their metamorphosis: Ametabola, Exopterygota and Endopterygota. The latter two names refer to the development – external and internal respectively – of the wings.

**AMETABOLA** This group includes the simplest and most primitive types of insect, such as fishmoths, that undergo virtually no change during growth other than in size, and none in habits. The young are just miniature adults.

**EXOPTERYGOTA** The young of these insects, called nymphs, look more or less like the adults except that they have no wings. The latter develop on the outside, becoming more distinct with each moult. They also share habitat and feeding habits with the adults. Cockroaches, praying mantids, stick insects, grasshoppers and bugs all belong in this group. Oddly enough so, too, do dragonflies and damselflies, whose young, known as naiads,

The external wing-buds of grasshopper nymphs are replaced by the fully developed wings of the adult.

A well-developed nymph of the grasshopper *Phymateus viridipes*. Note the external wing-buds.

look very different from their parents and live in a totally different environment: they are aquatic, the adults terrestrial. However, most importantly, they do not pass through an inactive pupal stage.

**ENDOPTERYGOTA** These species have young known as larvae, which are totally different from the adults in appearance, and usually differ in habits as well. Their wings develop internally, only becoming visible in the pupa – the resting stage between larva and adult that is characteristic of this group. The transformation from the larva to the adult takes place within the pupa, which is usually inactive, does not feed, and is often well hidden from predators. This group includes the antlions, beetles, flies, caddisflies, fleas, butterflies and moths, and ants, bees and wasps. In a few instances, even the larva assumes several different forms during its development, a phenomenon known as 'hypermetamorphosis'. Good examples of this are the mantid flies, whose freshly hatched larvae have well-developed legs and actively search for a spider's egg cocoon. Once inside, the larva starts feeding on the eggs or young spiders and moults into a fat, legless grub, which finally pupates when it is mature. Some blister beetles go through even more complicated hypermetamorphosis, passing through up to five different larval stages.

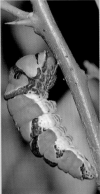

Mature larva.          About to pupate.

The pupa shows its silk girdle.

The newly emerged butterfly expands its wings.

About to hatch.

Emerging from the pupa.          The finished product: wings are fully expanded.

# THE SEARCH FOR FOOD

Some insects go to extraordinary lengths to get their food. Flies of the genus *Bengalia*, for example, hijack their meals: well camouflaged, they lie in ambush beside ant trails, monitoring passers-by, and when a laden ant comes along the fly will confront it head-on and snatch the load with its specially adapted proboscis. More often than not the fly is well rewarded by its blatant act of piracy, and retires to a quiet spot to enjoy the loot. Moreover, when a crowd of ants clusters around a large dead insect, one too big for a fly to carry away, it rivals a jackal in its boldness: hovering over the seething mass of preoccupied but potentially lethal ants, it dives in to retrieve any exposed morsel.

Most insects, however, are more conventional in their feeding habits, though many also employ intriguing and often quite complex strategies in their never-ending search for food.

**Left:** A hawk moth caterpillar feeds on the leaf of a white bristle bush. **Above:** Blowflies have lapping mouthparts designed for sucking up liquids.
**Top:** Grasshoppers are vegetarians; *Acanthacris* feeds voraciously on garden plants.

Insects can be divided into two broad groups: those that chew solid food and those that suck up liquids. Within each of these divisions there are species that feed on plants (herbivores), and those that feed on other animals (carnivores), either as predators or parasites. And then, of course, there are the scavengers. Such widely differing feeding habits have prompted fascinating modifications to the basic type of insect mouthparts (see box, page 17).

## Plant feeders

**THE CHEWING LIFESTYLE** Well over half of all insect species depend on plants – foliage for the most part – for their food. Equipped with strong mandibles, grasshoppers, stick insects, the caterpillars of butterflies and moths, many beetles, and the larvae of sawflies chew their way through mountainous quantities of leaves, sometimes with devastating effect on farm crops and garden plants. We all know, for instance, what locusts can do to a field of mealies.

Many leaf eaters are fully exposed while they feed, though most receive some protection from camouflage or deception or from their warning colours. Others, such as bagworms, make portable shelters or turn part of the leaf on which they are feeding into a protective shield. The larva of a skipper butterfly, for example, folds over the edge of a *Strelitzia* leaf and holds down the flap with silken pillars.

The larvae of some moths, beetles and flies, collectively known as 'leaf miners', feed within the actual leaves themselves. Of necessity these insects are small in size, flat in shape and therefore well adapted to their lifestyle. Although not easily visible themselves, their feeding galleries (or tunnels) are conspicuous signposts to their presence.

There are, of course, other plant parts that insects exploit. For example, cicada nymphs and the larvae of click beetles specialize on roots, and many beetles feed on fruit and flowers. Pollen is a valuable food source, collected by bees as provision for the young, or eaten by click, jewel and other beetles. In doing so, many insect species provide an important service by pollinating the plants. The larvae of some moths feed inside pods; others, such as the potato tuber moth, attack tubers.

Maize, wheat and other stored food grains attract various moths and beetles, among them the granary weevils and seed weevils. Seeds are equally at risk in the wild – a fact most graphically exemplified, perhaps, by the jumping bean moth *Empira melanobasis*. The moth larvae that infest the fallen seeds are so energetic that the 'bean' actually leaps about. Harvester ants also depend on seeds (mostly those of grasses), which the workers collect and store away in the granary cells of their nests.

Wood, dead or alive, might seem at first sight to be thoroughly unpalatable, but there are many beetles and other insects that make their living by boring in it, most of the larvae feeding on dead wood (including furniture). One would think that their presence deep inside the branch of a tree could create a waste disposal problem, but special adaptations invariably cope with this. For example yellow-headed borers, whose showy adults can be seen flying around in coastal bush and forest, make regular ejection holes as they tunnel steadily along a plant stem – which ends up looking somewhat like a flute.

Wood-boring moths, on the other hand, focus on living plants – and can cause extensive damage to their hosts. Resins oozing from tunnels in branches are evidence of goat moth caterpillars, while empty pupal cases protruding from tunnels show that the adults have already emerged.

Many termites also eat wood, finding the food either by building nests within dead branches or by foraging, often under the protective cover of those mud runways which one sees on trees and plants. Some species have a taste for man-made wooden structures. Harvester termites (Hodotermitidae), though, forage in open ground, collecting bits and pieces of vegetation to take back to the nest.

**SUCKING UP LIQUIDS** Numerous bugs of the order Hemiptera, both immature and adult, pierce plant tissues with their sharp probosces to tap the sap, and in so doing can introduce diseases or cause shoots to wither. Some of these insect species are known, aptly, as 'tip wilters'.

**Above:** A hoverfly *Asarkina* sp. drinks nectar from a flower. **Top:** The vegetarian ladybird *Epilachna paykulli*.

Aphids (or greenfly) are perhaps the most notorious of the sap suckers, taking in large volumes of sugar-rich fluid and excreting the excess, called honeydew. This is much savoured by ants and certain flies. The sticky substance can also cover the foliage, which is then colonized by sooty mould (a fungus) which turns the leaves black, disfiguring the plants and inhibiting photosynthesis. The nymphs of spittlebugs, on the other hand, dispose of excess plant sap by working it up into a froth that covers the whole insect, protecting it from both desiccation and predation: all that is visible on the plant is a glob of frothy liquid known as 'cuckoo spit'.

Another major plant food is nectar, a sugar-rich liquid found mostly in flowers – to which the insects are attracted visually. Many nectar feeders – butterflies and moths, certain flies, bees and wasps – pollinate the flowers they visit; most have mouthparts specially designed for sucking up the nectar, sometimes only from certain plant species. For example, those with short mouthparts cannot reach the nectar in long tubular flowers (unless they cheat by chewing through the base of the flower to reach the nectaries). Most remarkable of these specialist feeders are the tangle-veined flies, some species of which are blessed with proboscces up to four times the length of their bodies.

## Carnivores and bloodsuckers

**AMBUSH PREDATORS** Praying mantids are masters of the waiting game, standing motionless, beautifully camouflaged against plant stem, flower or foliage, invisible to predators and prey alike, and grabbing unwary passers-by with specially adapted forelegs – and with electrifying speed. Flower mantids are at a special advantage since, sooner or later, an insect is bound to visit the bloom they've staked out. Victims are held by the forelegs, in a vice-like grip, and systematically chewed up. In an extraordinary evolutionary vparallel, the unrelated mantid flies and some assassin bugs have forelegs almost identically modified for catching and holding prey.

The flower mantid in its colourful feeding ground.

Dragonfly and damselfly naiads, water bugs and water scorpions lurk about on aquatic plants waiting for unsuspecting insect larvae, tadpoles and small fish to come within reach (see pages 25 and 29). The water bugs and water scorpions, like the mantids, catch prey with their strongly developed raptorial forelegs, but pierce the victim's body with their sharp proboscces, injecting enzymes to dissolve the tissues so that they can be sucked out. The terrestrial assassin bugs and shield bugs employ the same technique.

Antlion larvae lie in wait in various situations, some just below the surface of the sand, from which their sickle-shaped mandibles will erupt when prey comes into range. The larvae of other antlion species take a more calculated approach: they excavate conical pits into which wandering insects will accidentally tumble. Once trapped, the insect cannot find enough purchase to climb out, and its escape is made even more difficult by the antlion, which hurls sprays of sand over it. Interestingly, the larvae of some flies, known as wormlions, have evolved the same technique. The larvae of owlflies, which are close relatives of the antlions, hide themselves on branches or among dead leaves and, having caught their prey, inject digestive enzymes into its body and suck out the resultant 'soup'.

**SEARCH-AND-PURSUE PREDATORS** Many other insects are less passive in their approach. Ground beetles and tiger beetles, for instance, run around in search of prey and, if necessary, give chase. Locating the prey is often helped by following its scent trail. Glow-worms, for example, follow the slime trails laid down by the snails and slugs they feed on; some bark beetles follow aerial scents.

Caterpillars of certain blue butterflies – including some in the subfamily Liphyrinae – feed on tree hoppers. The female simplifies the search by laying her eggs near a colony. By tending, or caressing, the hoppers in the same way as ants do in their quest for honeydew (see page 58), they gain the confidence of their victims. Other Liphyrinae species feed in similar fashion on scale insects. Ladybird beetles and lacewings, adults and larvae alike, capture aphids and other small insects in the same way.

Adult wasps generally feed on nectar and so, strictly speaking, are not predators. However, most female wasps act like predators because they have to hunt and catch prey for their young. And some use amazing strategies to do so. Digger wasps of the genus *Ammophila* are especially ingenious: they explore the ground beneath trees and bushes looking for fresh caterpillar droppings and, if these are there, fly up vertically to search among the foliage, methodically working their way to the top. The caterpillars' scent trails also help. Spider-hunting wasps, indeed, locate their victims largely by scent. Each kind of wasp, though, has its own technique, and there are probably as many different ways of finding and catching as there are species of prey.

Many kinds of ant are predatory, either exclusively or as part of a catholic diet that includes honeydew, nectar and other types of non-animal food. However, their social behaviour sets them apart from their fellow predators: the quest for food is a communal affair, many individuals searching more or less randomly. Large columns of driver or army ants, for instance, will comb an area, the workers fanning out in a broad front and attacking any living creature they encounter – an all-encompassing sweep that lays the area bare of food. The column soon has to move on, hence its nomadic lifestyle. Somewhat different in their approach are some of the ants of the subfamily Ponerinae, which prey on termites: they first send out scouts to locate the colonies, the successful scout laying a scent trail back to its nest and then leading a raiding column of its colleagues to the colony.

A hoverfly larva feeds voraciously on aphids.

Ant species with wider ranging tastes often capture insects they come across while they are foraging for other foods (tailor and pugnacious ants fall into this category). Others, such as the Pharaoh ant, send out lone scouts to find food; thief ants actually nest within termite mounds: their tunnels, too narrow for the larger termites, enable them to enter the colony, grab the eggs and brood and leave again, safe from pursuit.

**AERIAL PREDATORS** The most active of insect carnivores are those that catch their prey on the wing, either launching their attacks from a perch (robber flies, for example) or while in flight (swift-flying owlflies). Dragonflies and damselflies use both methods.

**Above:** The robber fly *Hoplistomerus nobilis* is a specialist, feeding on dung beetles. **Top:** The glade jewel, an especially striking damselfly, catches its insect prey on the wing.

Bee-wolves rely (initially at least) on their eyesight to locate the bees and wasps with which they provision their nests, some catching honey-bee workers at the hive entrances, others lurking near flowers that are attractive to bees, hovering downwind of a suitably sized victim and only seizing it after confirming its suitability by scent. Some species of the fly-catching genus *Bembix*

focus on horseflies: they fly around cattle, and swoop down on their victims in much the same way as a falcon catches a smaller bird in flight; others loiter with intent near cow pats.

**BLOODSUCKERS AND PARASITES** Broadly speaking there are two kinds of insects that suck blood from vertebrates, namely free-ranging and parasitic.

The adults of the first type live independently of their hosts except for sporadic visits to obtain blood, and consist mainly of flies of one sort or another, among them mosquitoes, biting midges, black flies, horseflies and tsetse flies. Apart from these last, only the females feed on blood (the males live on nectar), and they home in on their hosts by means of sight, smell and, in some cases, with the aid of heat radiating from the bodies of warm-blooded animals. Bedbugs are rather less independent but also visit their hosts only for meals. They emerge at night from hiding places in cracks in furniture, walls or floors and, guided by body heat and smell, feed on sleeping humans.

By contrast, the parasites – including sucking lice such as the human body louse – spend much the greater part of their lives living on or inside their hosts. Adult fleas are also parasitic, though their larvae scavenge away from the host's body. Among the few fly families to lead a parasitic life are the louseflies, bat flies and bat louseflies.

Bloodsucking horseflies are known to humans for their silent, and painful, attacks.

All parasitic insects that feed inside vertebrates are maggots of flies: the eggs, which are laid on the bodies or fur of their hosts, either hatch rapidly for the maggots to bore through the skin, or are licked off by the host and swallowed. Parasitism by fly maggots, whether internal or external, is called 'myiasis'.

**INSECT PARASITES** The bloodsuckers and parasites discussed above rarely kill their hosts; parasites that attack other insects often do. Known as parasitoids, they are mainly the larvae of wasps and flies together with a few beetles, and include both internal- and external-feeding species. The adults help their offspring locate a food source by depositing eggs or young larvae on or near a suitable host.

**UNUSUAL PREDATORS** In their early stages the caterpillars of some blue butterflies (family Lycaenidae) feed on foliage, and are attended by ants for the honeydew they produce. At first they prevent the ants from moving them, but after the

## Scavengers

**FEEDERS ON EXCREMENT** Many insects scavenge on animal excrement and other organic waste. The adults and larvae of flesh flies, blowflies, house flies and their relatives feed on the liquids of fresh faeces. Adult dung beetles also drink the liquids but their larvae include solids in their diet. Even some butterflies stray from their more traditional diet of nectar and can be seen sucking up liquids from dung and, more rarely, from carcasses.

**DRINKING HONEYDEW** Caterpillars of blue butterflies and sap-feeding insects such as scale insects, tree hoppers and the previously mentioned aphids (see page 54) excrete excess liquids, taken up from their host plants, in the form of honeydew – a substance rich in nutrients and sugars that attracts ants. In return for the food, the ants will protect these insects from parasites and predators. Some butterflies are also drawn to the feast. One in particular, known as 'woolly legs', attends groundnut hoppers, stroking them with

Ants attending the larva of a lycaenid butterfly.

second moult they allow themselves to be carried back to the nests, where they begin feeding on the silk of the ants' cocoons. They then turn carnivorous, eating the pupae as well. Amazingly, the ants do nothing to stop them.

**SPECIALIZED FEEDING HABITS** Unlike bees' nests, those of the ants have no cells for storing honey. Some ants rely on living 'larders' instead. *Anoplolepis trimeni*, for example, feeds nectar and honeydew to special workers, known as repletes, that hang from the roof of the nest chamber. The repletes swell up to an enormous size, serving as storage containers from which the 'honey' can be retrieved at any time by the workers.

An African monarch *Danaus chrysippus* visiting dung; some butterflies supplement their nectar diet with fluids from excrement.

Ants of the genus *Polyrachis* attend tree hoppers for their honeydew.

its antennae to elicit the honeydew. Its unusually hairy legs and body are perhaps a defence against the ants alongside which it finds itself feeding.

**EATING DEAD PLANT MATERIAL** Numbered among this type of feeder are the larvae of crane flies, snipe flies, robber flies, soldier flies, scarab and click beetles, the naiads of mayflies, the young and adults of fishmoths and, of course, the wood borers mentioned earlier (see page 54).

**EATING DEAD ANIMALS** Freshly dead and decaying bodies of other animals attract many flies and beetles. Flesh- and blowflies are among the first to deposit their eggs or larvae on newly killed meat; carrion and rove beetles are attracted at a later stage of decay, while hide beetles, trox beetles and species of the clothes moth family (Tineidae) specialize in dried carcasses, skin, feathers and bones. Hide beetles, in fact, provide a minor but useful service to science: they are sometimes employed to clean delicate skeletons for study and museum display.

Relatively few insects feed on the dead remains of other insects. Notorious, though, is the museum beetle *Anthrenus verbasci* which can devastate poorly cared-for insect collections stored in cabinet drawers.

## Omnivores

These insects eat just about any organic matter they can find. Cockroaches are renowned for their non-discerning appetites – eating habits that allow them to thrive in those slightly less than hygienic houses where bits and pieces of food are left lying around. Most fishmoths and the larvae of fleas are also omnivorous, the latter eating both animal and vegetable debris found in the resting places of their hosts.

Ants are the only members of the order Hymenoptera that scavenge – and, because they are also predatory, are perhaps the most strikingly omnivorous of all. Especially impressive is a broad column of army ants on the move.

# THE SOCIAL INSECTS

**Above:** Termite hills, of the *Trinervitermes* species, dot the Eastern Cape countryside. **Left:** A typical nest of the paper wasp *Ropalidia* sp.

These insect communities rank among the wonders of nature. As we have already seen (pages 26, 38–41), they include the termites and ants, all of which are social, and some of the bees and wasps.

Ants and termites have evolved, quite independently of each other, a very similar type of social organization – which is a quite extraordinary phenomenon, because termites are descended from a type of cockroach while the ancestors of ants were primitive wasps.

## Architects supreme

Termites are the most conspicuous of all the social insects because of the enormous structures that many species erect above their subterranean nests, earthen hills that are a notable feature of many a tropical and subtropical landscape. Some of the larger ones may contain several tons of soil, all carried up laboriously from below, particle by particle, by battalions of small blind workers. The inhabitants of a single colony may number into the millions and, most remarkably, they are all brothers and sisters, the offspring of the male and female that founded the colony.

With so many living together in a confined space, the insects must overcome the problems posed by a build-up of heat, especially in summer, and of carbon dioxide. They do so by designing air-conditioned homes – mounds within which the air circulates (see box, page 62).

## How Termites Keep Cool

Termite hills vary greatly in size and complexity according to the species. However, a look at one of the more sophisticated structures illustrates just how the residents manage to control the interior temperature.

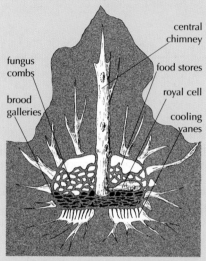

Cross section of a termite mound.

Air in the nest chambers, heated and depleted of oxygen by the energy expended by the occupants, rises, flowing up a central chimney and into thin-walled ventilation flues just below the surface of the mound's outer wall. Here an exchange of carbon dioxide and oxygen, together with some cooling of the air, takes place. Pressurized by heat rising from below, the rejuvenated air then flows down other passageways into the cavities below the nest chambers, passing through specially constructed vanes, which are kept damp by the termites. This cools the air further before it passes back into the nest chambers.

That such remarkably intricate, fully air-conditioned structures can be built by tiny, delicate and blind insects seems little short of miraculous.

Day-to-day activities are controlled automatically by a remarkable system of communication, one based largely on chemical messages. The system ensures that all aspects of the colony's life, and the stability of environmental conditions within the colony, are properly regulated. Personal contact is the key to success: workers lay scent trails to newly found sources of food for others to follow, and exchange food, saliva and anal excretions with one another. They also feed on each others' droppings, extracting every last bit of nourishment. Workers feed the queen, the king, the nymphs and soldiers. They also groom the queen, and take drops of anal liquid from her.

This ceaseless, frenetic interchange guarantees that a number of crucial chemicals (pheromones) circulates among all the members of the colony. Changes in the proportions of the pheromones trigger appropriate changes in behaviour, restoring and sustaining equilibrium. For instance, a decline in soldier numbers reduces the amount of soldier pheromone in the food being fed to the queen, which prompts her to produce more soldiers. In much the same way the development of sterile, wingless workers is controlled by a pheromone produced by the queen and fed to the nymphs. Soldiers maintain a rather less sophisticated, but effective, method of communication – an alarm system – by tapping on the walls of the tunnels.

A flight of tasty termites attracts predators of many kinds, including frogs.

At certain times of the year, a change in the termite queen's pheromones heralds the appearance of winged males and females. When conditions are just right, usually after heavy rain, they pour out of specially prepared and guarded exits in their thousands to pair up, mate and found new colonies. These are the familiar flights of so-called 'flying ants'. After a short journey they come to ground, shed their wings and, having found a mate, proceed in tandem to look for a suitable nest site, the male doggedly following the female nose to tail. Many are killed before they reach their destination, their nutritious bodies eagerly snapped up by a horde of hungry birds, lizards, frogs and other predators – not to mention rural folk with a taste for fried 'ants'.

## Simple beginnings

The social organization and nest architecture of the ants and the social bees and wasps are equal to those of the termites. However, one must not ignore the efforts of the many solitary species of bees and wasps, lone creatures which construct simple or multiple nests and whose behaviour is thought to represent the evolutionary steps that led to social life in the first place. In fact, social behaviour has developed quite independently at least eleven times within the world of the ants, bees and wasps.

The elaborate nest turret of the spider-hunting wasp *Dichragenia pulchricoma*.

Burrows in the ground cannot really be regarded as architecture. Once completed they are most often simply sealed and abandoned, leaving very few visible signs of their presence. Some species, though, nest in clay soil, which they soften with regurgitated water, and build turrets over the burrow entrances from the excavated mud-pellets. These turrets vary in design from species to species, and in some cases may serve as protection against nest parasites, though their real function is not fully understood. Often, too, species that nest in hollow twigs or cavities in wood construct turrets at the

This mason wasp is pushing a paralysed caterpillar into its nest.

The six-sided cells of a *Polistes* wasp's paper nest. It contains grubs at various stages of development.

entrances; some erect partitions between the nest cells, very often from mud but sometimes from vegetable material (in which case there are no turrets). The leaf-cutter bees are notable interior designers, cutting discs from living leaves to line and partition their nests. Species of *Creightoniella*, on the other hand, produce an extremely tough material by scraping wood pulp from the bark of trees and combining it with resin.

Real architecture is created by solitary wasps that build nests above ground. These are invariably moulded out of mud and may be simple one- or two-celled jobs or much larger structures of numerous cells. Some wasps build several one-celled mud nests within a single cavity, either in branches or rocks. Females emerging from these mate and go on to construct more nests in the same cavity, next door to their mother who, being long-lived, carries on associating with her young. Indeed, as her reproductive powers dwindle, she may even take up guard duty – and here we have the early beginnings of social behaviour.

Building individual aerial nests seems less common among the bees, but some attach one-celled nests of wood pulp to tree trunks, or many-celled resinous nests to rocks, embedding a myriad small stones into the fabric. Carpenter bees make up one of four tribes in the subfamily Xylocopinae and are known for the large holes they drill, often in timber structures (which can cause considerable damage). Females place their cells end to end in the burrows and vigorously defend the nests against intruders. But there is still no sign of social life.

However, several species of another tribe, consisting of the allodapine bees, burrow in pithy stems but do not make individual cells for their young. The larvae develop together, and are fed by the mother. The first females to emerge care for their younger siblings, and there is the hint of a caste system – the very beginnings of social life – in the size differential between the queen and the female workers (the former is slightly larger than the latter).

Sweat bees of the family Halictidae excavate nest burrows in the ground or in rotting wood, and some species are semi-social: the older female and her brood of males and workers live together. In other species, individuals co-operate in nest construction; in still others the females simply share a common entrance to otherwise separate nests.

## Social outcomes among wasps

The familiar paper wasps represent the highest level of social life among southern African wasps. These relatively primitive social wasps build their nests with 'paper' made from a mixture of wood scrapings and saliva, attached to the substrate by a stalk or pedicel which is coated with an ant repellent. The nests, commonly seen hanging from roof beams, and sometimes from tree trunks, are made up of one or more combs of six-sided cells and come in a variety of shapes. They are quite small but vary greatly in size, averaging around 50 cells though there can be as many as 200. However, they are not nearly so diverse or complex as the nests of their relatives in other parts of the world.

Nest-building is initiated by mated females, either singly or in a small group surviving from the previous season. In a group effort, one member quickly establishes her dominance and does most of the egg-laying while her subordinates handle the other tasks. No pheromones are needed to control their activities because the colony is small enough (it seldom exceeds 100 members) to be regulated by straightforward physical dominance.

Subordinates in the group-originated colonies start to die or leave the nest when the first adults emerge. These are mostly females who look much like their mother, and who become workers, taking over all the colony duties – including defence and the gathering of nectar or insect food. Among the latter, caterpillars are a favoured item, collected on foraging expeditions, chewed to pulp and shared with nestmates and grubs. Especially interesting is the way the grubs produce droplets of liquid from their mouths, a substance eagerly taken up by workers – perhaps a gesture of appeasement by the grubs since there is a tendency to cannibalism within wasp communities, most commonly before the emergence of the first adults. Later in the season, males and non-working reproductive females are produced, after which the colony starts going into decline. The nest is finally abandoned, males and females leaving to mate. The males will then die. The females spend the winter or dry season in sheltered spots, sometimes in large aggregations.

## Home life among the bees

Social organization in this group reaches its greatest development in the family Apidae, which includes the honeybees and stingless bees.

Stingless bees, more commonly called mopane bees, nest in tree and rock hollows, each colony complete with its queen, workers and males, the whole totalling a few hundred individuals. Separate areas are set aside for the brood and honey or pollen storage, and the entrance is fitted with a wax and resin tube, which is guarded during the day by workers. Mopane bees can cause real discomfort to humans through their habit of seeking moisture from the eyes.

A paper wasp, *Belonogaster brachystoma,* pulverizing its caterpillar prey.

# DANCE OF THE HONEYBEE

A worker honeybee returning to the hive will inform fellow workers of the quality, distance from the hive and direction of a food source by means of a ritualized 'dance'. This is performed in the dark, on the vertical combs, and is 'watched' by her worker audience.

If the food source is quite close, the bee does a series of circular runs with regular changes of direction. The frequency of these changes indicates the quality of the food. Information on direction is unnecessary when the food is close by.

For more distant food sources, the bee will dance as shown in the illustration. The number of 'tail' wags during the straight run of the dance indicates the distance, while the angle of the straight run to the left or right of the vertical indicates direction – at what angle the food lies to the left or right of the sun.

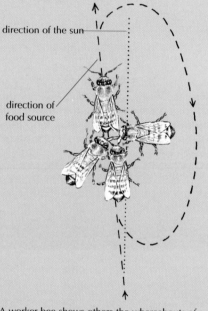

direction of the sun

direction of food source

A worker bee shows others the whereabouts of a source of nectar by means of a 'dance'.

The honeybee *Apis mellifera* has a much more advanced social organization. Members number in their tens of thousands, and there are very pronounced differences between the queen, the male and the worker caste. The workers, which are underdeveloped females, carry out all the tasks required to maintain the colony, including cleaning, ventilating the hive, collecting water, feeding larvae, storing food, ripening the honey, guarding, foraging, and producing the wax used to build combs (which is done with extraordinary precision). Each worker progresses through the range of duties during her lifetime.

Most fascinating is the dance given by a honeybee worker to tell her co-workers the direction and distance of a newly discovered food source (see box, above).

The queen's sole task is to lay eggs in wax cells that are prepared by the workers. She also produces a pheromone-containing substance which the workers obtain by licking her body, and which is circulated throughout the colony through the exchange of food between workers. The substance prevents them building rival queen cells, and stops the development of workers into egg-laying castes.

## Ants: the premier social insects

The most advanced and complex form of social life within the insect world is to be found among the ants. These little creatures are also the most widespread and abundant, both generally and in the size of their communities: a colony, especially that of driver (or army) ants, may run into the millions. They are also a remarkably diverse group, both in their nesting habits and in their diet. Some species are carnivorous, others granivorous (seed and grain eaters), many are omnivores.

Ants' nests may not be as conspicuous as those of termites, but they're generally every bit as extensive and even more diverse, though some species (notably the driver ants) have no fixed abode. The variety is bewildering; here, we can touch on just a few examples. The aerial nests of tailor and cocktail ants have already been mentioned (see pages 10 and 41). Ants of the subfamily Pseudomyrmecinae build their smallish nests in hollow twigs, reeds or thorns, notably those of acacia trees, and defend them vigorously. Some species construct subterranean nests that can penetrate to a depth of six metres or more, with little showing on the surface to indicate their presence. Those of ponerine ants have a simple

The distinctive carton nests of some cocktail ants are made from chewed vegetable matter.

entrance in the ground surrounded by a mound. Members of the subfamily Myrmicinae nest below stones, marking the entrances with loose soil carried out by the workers. Heaps of grass are signposts to the nest entrances of harvester ants, and those that nest in the hollows of tree trunks and branches reduce the size of the opening with pieces of grass and other vegetation.

The ant caste system is similar in many ways to that of the termites, encompassing workers, sometimes of more than one type, and soldiers. Like the termites, these are sterile but, by contrast, all are female and adult. There are other major organizational differences between the two groups. For instance the young of ants, which are helpless grubs unable to contribute to the colony's activities, are fed and otherwise cared for by workers. The queen (usually just one) is also nurtured by the workers but, unlike the termite social structure, there is no male in attendance.

Winged ant males and females are produced at certain times of the year and, when conditions are favourable, they make their way out through special flight holes. Like that of the termites, the nuptial flight is short, the male (unusually large in some species) dies, and the mated female straightaway looks for a suitable nesting site. She then drops her wings, prepares the beginning of a nest and starts to lay eggs. Until she has produced the first workers, she must live off her own body reserves, though the queens of some primitive ant groups forage for their own food.

The success of an ant colony also depends on communication, either physical or, more importantly, chemical, between the members. Pheromones sound the alarms and attract other workers to the source of trouble, and a sufficiently high chemical concentration will trigger aggressiveness. Some ants use sound – warning 'chirps' generated by the movement of segments of the abdomen – to the same effect. Worker ants also lay odour trails leading others to newly discovered sources of food or new nest sites. Sight can also play a role in recruitment – those ants with large eyes respond to the movements of other colony members and join up with them in working parties.

# STRATEGIES FOR SURVIVAL

Insects are a major source of food for a vast array of birds, mammals, reptiles and amphibians – and for a great many parasites and predators from among their own kind. That they have survived to become the most abundant, and widespread, animals on earth is a tribute to their extraordinarily diverse range of defensive capabilities.

## Robustness

The insect's external skeleton, which has enabled it to develop a tough cuticle, gives it pretty effective protection against predator attack. Anyone who collects insects and has tried to push a pin through a jewel beetle will bear witness to just how strong the casing can be. Moreover, the streamlined shape and smoothness of these beetles render them slippery, difficult to grasp. Indeed many ground-dwelling beetles, such as lily weevils, are surprisingly robust, potential meals only for the larger and better equipped predators. Certain wasps, cuckoo wasps and velvet ants (these are also wasps) are amazingly strong as well. All these insects are seemingly quite confident in their security and make very little effort to hide themselves.

Heavily armoured insects, among them certain caterpillars (notably those of emperor moths) and some of the larger grasshoppers, often supplement their defences with spines, For instance *Acanthacris*, often found in gardens, has rows of formidable spines – which can draw blood if the insect is carelessly handled – on its powerful hindlegs. Armoured ground crickets are doubly blessed, combining sharp spines on the thorax with a repellent fluid.

Having said that, though, robustness is by no means a watertight guarantee against predation. For example many well-armoured beetles, the larger of which tend to be rather clumsy and not very mobile, are eaten by birds of prey, bats and the smaller mammalian carnivores.

## Agility and awareness

Houseflies are notoriously adept at avoiding capture, and grasshoppers can take off in a split second. Tiger beetles are also extraordinarily difficult to catch: they run quickly, and take to the air in instant flight. Many less agile insects reverse the strategy: when they sense the approach of an

**Left:** The common emperor moth caterpillar is armed with defensive spines. **Above:** The spines on the hind tibia (or 'shinbone') of the grasshopper *Acanthacris*. **Top:** The warning colours of a blister beetle *Mylabris oculata*.

The agility of the tiger beetle *Cicindela brevicollis* is the key to its survival.

animal, even the mere passing of a shadow, some beetles will drop from their resting places on plants and remain motionless. Ground-dwellers such as lily weevils and tok-tokkie beetles feign death when attacked.

Click beetles are agile in a quite different and novel way. Like many other hard-shelled creatures (including tortoises) they have difficulty getting back on their feet when they find themselves on their backs, but this particular insect is helped by an ingenious catapult-type mechanism. It arches its back, engages a special spine in a notch on its underside and then, with an audible click, spine and notch disengage to arch the body in the opposite direction, throwing the beetle into the air. With luck, it lands on its feet. It also uses the mechanism to escape the grip of a predator.

## Camouflage

This is perhaps the most common defensive weapon in the insect world. A simple colour-match between a species and its normal background is basic to successful concealment – but often it isn't enough: insects are three dimensional, showing up in relief and casting give-away shadows. They also tend to be symmetrical, displaying a shape or outline that is alien to their surroundings.

So some of them have evolved compensations. Certain caterpillars, for example, eliminate the three-dimensional perspective with countershading: that part of the caterpillar's body that habitually faces the light is darker, counteracting the brighter lighting and effectively making the insect appear to be flat – an obvious advantage to leaf-dwellers. Dealing with shadows is more complicated and calls for structural modifications to the body. Among these are rows of bristles or other protuberances which effectively bridge the give-away gap between body and branch.

Then there is what is known as 'disruptive coloration'. Backgrounds are seldom uniform, varying from place to place and under different lighting conditions. As a result, an unbroken symmetrical shape – for example the triangular outline of a moth at rest – may be fairly easily recognized in spite of what would otherwise be an excellent disguise. Consequently, many species display bold, abstract patterns that divert attention from the shape, breaking it up into a number of irregular and apparently separate units.

## Deception

A more complex form of camouflage is to imitate a commonly found inedible object, a ploy which, to be successful, often demands major changes in body structure and behaviour. For instance looper caterpillars, so called from the way they loop their bodies when walking, have lost three of the usual five pairs of false legs on the abdomen, and have added a variety of protuberances to the body that resemble dormant buds or irregularities on bark, and, when they adopt the correct posture, are indistinguishable from twigs. Similarly,

**Above:** This caterpillar's bristles obscure its give-away shadow. **Above right:** A leaf-mimicking katydid.

the caterpillar of the pearl spangled moth mimics the stump of a broken twig, even down to the fine black lines that pass for cracks in the bark.

But it is the stick insects that have taken deception to the limits of credibility. An encounter with one of the very large species, which reach some 250 mm in length, is little short of awe-inspiring: the entire body, including legs and wings, contributes to the transformation of the ungainly creature into a perfect 'stick'. The body is decorated with tubercles and spines that look just like the thorns and stumps of broken twigs, and the whole is virtually impossible to distinguish from its natural surroundings. Mantids come a close second: they are cryptically coloured, and in many cases their bodies and legs are adorned with various extensions that complete the camouflage.

Some beetles and grasshoppers, those that live on bare, stony ground, not only have the colour of the stones but have also taken on their square or rounded shapes. Bird droppings are often found on leaves, but one must look closely to discern that they are not young swallowtail caterpillars in disguise. Some butterflies, moths and grasshoppers pass themselves off as leaves, complete with 'veins' and even convincingly 'nibbled' holes. Various beetles mimic seeds, treehoppers pretend to be thorns, and so on. There are endless examples.

Not all kinds of deception, though, involve major body modifications. The nymphs of some assassin bugs, for example, just cover themselves with particles of soil, vegetation or other debris from their habitat; the larvae of tortoise beetles blanket themselves with their own caste larval skins and excreta.

Especially intriguing are the portable cases made by the larvae of caddisflies and bagworms. Those of the bagworms are built from sticks or pieces of leaves or grass held together with extremely tough silk and are very difficult to open. The bagworm wanders about feeding on foliage, carrying its 'home' with it, and at the first sign of danger it freezes, pulling the structure over its head. Some species make beautifully camouflaged cases, those of thorn bagworms incredibly accurate replicas of acacia thorns; others have

The young larvae of the citrus swallowtail butterfly disguise themselves as bird droppings.

fairly conspicuous cases but it is not obvious to a predator what they are, nor that a meal is to be found inside. In spite of this there is a wasp of the family Eumenidae that provisions its nest entirely with the larvae of bagworms, but just how it extricates them from their bags remains a mystery. The aquatic larvae of caddisflies are even more inventive: they use twigs, leaf fragments, small stones or sand grains to construct cases that can withstand a wide range of underwater conditions.

## Adaptive behaviour

However perfect the camouflage or deception, it will only work if the insect behaves appropriately. Movement is the greatest of give-aways, and it cannot of course be avoided entirely, so caterpillars and stick insects will freeze at the slightest disturbance, taking up a pose that makes best use of their disguise.

Other insects remain motionless during the day, taking full advantage of their camouflage, and confine their feeding and other activities to the dark hours, when there are fewer predators abroad and movement is not so easily discerned. Most moths are nocturnal, spending the day at

The looper caterpillars of the family Geometridae are uncannily stick-like.

rest and well camouflaged. Many caterpillars also employ this strategy; some have an extra means of defence: chewed foliage can attract the attention of predators, so when the insects are not feeding they move to another part of the plant.

## The collective effort

Less commonly, several individuals co-operate in the deception exercise. Various plant bugs feed in clusters, creating the impression of an inflorescence (an arrangement of flowers on a stalk), even grading themselves according to colour so as to perfect the illusion. The larvae of long-horned antlions remain grouped around their empty eggshells – the eggs are laid on plant stems – for a day or two before they disperse so that, for a time, they resemble some kind of dry seed-head rather than a tasty morsel.

emit a loud (and intimidating) rustling sound when suddenly opened. Short-horned grasshoppers also make good use of this technique. When disturbed they take off abruptly and, while in flight, show off their brightly coloured hindwings. But just before plunging into a new resting place the wings are suddenly closed, switching off the colours so that it appears the insect has completely vanished! Some long-horned grasshoppers, by contrast, do not resort to flight but display their wings to expose the bright colours of the abdomen while, at the same time, exuding noxious liquids.

Praying mantids need both to conceal themselves from prey and to defend themselves from enemies so, apart from their excellent camouflage, many species have developed bright colours on their hindwings and raptorial forelegs that are

Owlfly larvae resemble a seed head as they cluster above their empty eggshells.

The bush locust *Phymateus morbillosus* will flash its bright hindwings to discourage a molester.

## Flash coloration

Many well-camouflaged winged insects have brightly coloured or patterned hindwings which are hidden by the forewings when they are resting. This provides them with a second line of defence, which comes into play when their disguises fail. Suddenly opening wings in preparation for flight automatically exposes the hindwings, either startling the predator or diverting its attention to less vulnerable parts of the insect's body. Large stick insects can put on an especially impressive display – although their wings are not particularly brightly coloured, they

used actively in threat displays. Indeed they even strike out at their attackers with their forelegs.

Not all winged insects are capable of instant flight. Some may be weak fliers; others first have to warm up their flight muscles and need to play for time. Here, cryptic coloration sometimes gives way to designs that resemble huge eyes – a notable feature of certain emperor moths. The 'eyes' are usually on the hindwings which, when danger threatens, suddenly open to reveal their threatening glare. The predator hesitates, and the moth has time to prepare itself for take-off. Other insects have developed variations on the theme:

A snap at the 'head' of this blue butterfly will yield a mouthful of hindwing!

This assassin bug shares the warning colours of the cotton stainers that feature in its diet.

one species of praying mantid displays a circular eye-like pattern on each of the forewings, which are spread out to face the attacker; the cream striped owl moth has eyespots permanently displayed on its forewings, which are flicked up to draw immediate attention to the two staring eyes on a dark-brown 'face'. Caterpillars of some species of hawk moth have one or two, sometimes more, pairs of 'eyes' on their front segments, which are inflated, displaying the stare to full advantage, when the insect rears up and retracts its head.

## Confusing the predator

Some butterflies, especially those of the family Satyridae, have smaller eyespots – near the edges of their wings – which serve to draw attention away from more vulnerable parts of the body and which tend to be targeted, so that the butterfly will often escape from an attack relatively unscathed. Other insects exploit the tendency for predators to strike at their heads by developing false heads. Some blues, for example, have thin antenna-like tails and accompanying eyespots at the tips of the hindwings. The butterfly draws attention to the 'head' by moving its hindwings, and hence the 'antennae' and 'eyes', up and down, especially just after alighting.

## Lethal weapons

Ants, bees and wasps sting – or rather, the females of these insects do, by means of ovipositors modified either for paralysing prey or for self defence, or both. Stinging involves the injection of a venom (this, rather than the puncture, causes the actual pain or paralysis). In social species the venom is specifically for defence, and therefore results in an especially painful sting. Colonies of social paper

wasps, for example, are feared by anyone who is familiar with them, and it is significant that certain birds, such as bronze mannikins and blue waxbills, will build their nests near such colonies in order to enjoy some protection from predators. Stings of solitary wasps, on the other hand, are used mostly for paralysing the prey they provide for their larvae, but they can also be put to good effect in self-defence by some species. Similarly, predator assassin bugs have evolved toxic saliva, containing nerve poisons and digestive enzymes, which they inject into their prey via a needle-sharp proboscis that is readily and most effectively used in self-defence as well. Some beetles have particularly strong, sharp madibles capable of giving an effective nip. Certain of the bigger praying mantids and crickets (and especially the large *Clonia wahlbergi*) will also bite if provoked. These are all predatory species whose mandibles are primarily for catching or chewing up their victims.

This caterpillar of the slugmoth family Limacodidae can deliver a painful sting.

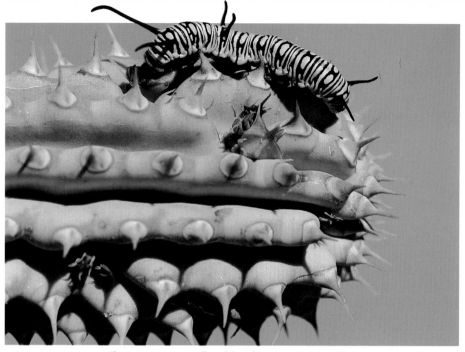

The poisonous caterpillar of the African monarch butterfly.

## Stinging hairs and spines

One tends to be wary of hairy caterpillars, perhaps because of nasty childhood experiences. If handled, their hairs puncture the skin and break off, leaving a burning sensation or an itching rash (caused by the body's release of histamine in response to the injected poison). Most predatory birds avoid them, though they do seem to attract cuckoos. Typical examples are the 'woolly bear' caterpillars of tiger moths, which are so often seen crossing roads, and those of various tussock and eggar moths.

The long hairs of this eggar moth caterpillar conceal the presence of short, poisonous spines.

Lappet moth larvae are somewhat flattened, with lateral tufts of hairs which are part of their camouflage, covering the gap between the body and the branch they are resting on. Hidden on the thoracic segments are tufts of colourful erectile spines that can be displayed as a warning signal. Any attempt to touch the caterpillar prompts it to flick its head from side to side, increasing the likelihood of making contact. The defence provided by such hairs is often passed on to later stages in the life cycle: the hairs may be incorporated into the cocoon, for instance, or even become attached to the emerging moth, where they retain their stinging properties.

The most notorious stinging caterpillars are those of the slugmoths, rather squat larvae equipped with tufts of sharp spines, often arranged on fleshy tubercles, that cause intense pain on contact (which need be no more than a fleeting touch). Large numbers of one species, *Latoia vivida*, sometimes accumulate in coffee plantations, other species on various fruit trees, and may interfere with the harvesting.

## Colours and chemicals

Anyone who has tried to pick up a velvet ant (which is actually a wingless female of the wasp family Mutillidae) will know how effectively some insects can defend themselves, and also learn the meaning of warning colours. Its red thorax and domino-like black-and-white pattern on the abdomen are instantly recognizable, and will become a vivid reminder of a painful experience. Thereafter, one harbours a healthy respect for any insect with the same or similar colouring. In fact it's usually safe to assume that insects displaying any bright colours and bold patterns have something unpleasant – either a sting or the ingredients of chemical warfare – to offer.

The bright colours of the grasshopper *Dictyophorus spumans* warn of the unpleasant foam it produces.

Large, fast-moving ground beetles are a common sight during the summer months as they run around in search of prey. They themselves have little to fear from predators: they are masters of chemical defence, able to squirt liquids containing acids (carried in special glands at the rear of the abdomen) at attackers over some distance and with some accuracy. Bombardier beetles and ants' nest beetles have gone one step further: they have developed explosive devices – a cloud of hot corrosive hydroquinones is expelled, with an audible explosive reaction, from a special 'combustion' chamber near the tip of the abdomen. More commonly, though, such conspicuous insects exude toxic or smelly fluids or simply taste repulsive.

Most moths are nocturnal and modestly marked, but not all: some are very brightly coloured and fly nonchalantly around in broad daylight, advertising their distastefulness. Blister beetles are particularly nasty – their bodies contain cantharidin, a powerful blistering agent which can be fatal if swallowed. Rove beetles secrete a corrosive liquid containing pederin, which also causes severe blistering if the insects are crushed against the skin. Notable among such are small red-and-blue species of *Paederus*, known as Nairobi eye flies. Ladybird beetles exude, from their leg joints, a yellow, very bitter fluid that contains alkaloids that are known to be toxic to birds and other animals. Just how poisonous some insects are is well illustrated by the traditional Bushmen, who tip their lethal hunting arrows with venom extracted from the larvae of *Diamphidia* beetles.

Shield bugs and tip wilters are aptly known as 'stink bugs' (see page 30), exuding a fluid with an extremely powerful, obnoxious smell which some species can squirt for several centimetres. Occasionally certain of the smaller shield bugs, such as *Carbula*, collect together in huge numbers to spend the dry season in a sheltered place – under bark, for instance, in rock crevices and even in someone's house, much to the annoyance of the occupants. Such swarms of smelly bugs can be of spectacular proportions in Zimbabwe's Hwange National Park and Kariba areas, and have to be destroyed and removed in bucket loads!

The inflated osmeterium (the fork-like organ behind its head) of this citrus swallowtail caterpillar gives off a repugnant smell.

Brightly coloured insects such as the elegant grasshopper and bush locusts, of the family Pyrgomorphidae, confidently flaunt their presence and fan out their gaudy hindwings when they are threatened and, if the attacker persists, will supplement the defensive display with an evil-smelling frothy liquid (see page 75).

Butterflies and moths also indulge in chemical warfare, both as caterpillars and as adults, sometimes even in the egg stage, and the toxins and repellents seem to be even more diverse than in other insects. Monarch caterpillars hijack poisonous cardenolides from their food plants to store them in their bodies, where they remain active, persisting into the adult stage; acraeas exude foul-tasting yellow liquids rich in hydrocyanic acid; the caterpillars of swallowtail butterflies have a bright-red, forked, tubular structure concealed behind the head known as the 'osmeterium' which, when the insect is disturbed, is turned inside out to emit a repugnant smell.

There is a bewildering variety of such chemically armed insects, but most have one thing in common: conspicuous patterns and bright colours – often yellow, orange, green or red, set off against black – which act as a warning to predators. The effectiveness of this 'aposematic' coloration depends, though, on the predators learning to keep their distance.

## Mimicry

This is a form of deception in which one insect, the mimic, takes on the appearance of another species that displays warning colours as protection against predators. The mimic is often, though not always, both harmless and tasty (this is called Batesian mimicry), and generally speaking its coloration will prove effective only so long as it remains far fewer in number than its model. Predators learn by trial and error which insects are edible, so if a mimic becomes too common, a larger proportion of the prey will be palatable and the predator will be less likely to recognize the colour pattern as a warning.

Butterflies provide particularly striking illustrations of mimicry. Their large wings are ideal, uniformly-shaped canvasses for the display of

**THE MASTER MIMIC**

The mocker swallowtail, *Papilio dardanus*, has evolved a highly original defensive ploy. The male is pictured at the top; the three different female forms on the left hand side mimic three quite different, distasteful butterflies of the family Danaidae, seen on the right.

colours and patterns. Among the best known examples is the mocker swallowtail (family Papilionidae), whose females occur in several distinct forms, each mimicking a different model. In other insects successful mimicry usually requires more than just a close copy of colour patterns: body shape and behaviour are also important.

A close-up look at models and mimics in a collection may not be all that convincing, since the mimicry will be at its best when the insects are observed alive, in their natural habitat. For instance, some robber flies in flight are remarkably good mimics of bees and wasps; indeed the large black and red *Proagonistes* species are, to us humans at least, almost indistinguishable from some spider-hunting wasps, though at rest their differences are more apparent. However, it is presumably when they are flying that they are most likely to be attacked. On the other hand another robber fly, *Hyperechia marshalli*, is remarkably similar to a carpenter bee, even as a specimen in a collection. In both cases, successful impersonation is conferred by body shape and hairiness as well as colour.

We have already seen (page 75) how well velvet ants, which are ground-dwelling wasps, defend themselves. One insect that takes advantage of the velvet ant's distinctive appearance to cash in on its reputation is a ground beetle (family Carabidae). There are clear similarities in colour pattern, and when the beetle runs across open ground, few predators familiar with velvet ants dare try to catch it. Then there's a wasp (*Osprynchotus*) that parasitizes the nest of another wasp, the well-known and strikingly coloured black and yellow mud-dauber. The parasite is almost indistinguishable from its host, especially in flight, and apparently enjoys immunity from predators even though it has no sting.

Mimicry, though, may be more than just a simple protection from enemies. Some predatory insects mimic their prey, presumably to allow them to approach easily. But here one ought to be cautious in coming to conclusions before the facts are known. For example cotton stainers, which are distinctively marked bugs that feed on the seeds of cotton and other related plants, are preyed upon by a similar looking assassin bug, but it turns out that this has nothing to do with stealth. Here the warning pattern is shared by two distasteful species (Mullerian mimicry), an arrangement that gets the message across more quickly: the common predator has to learn just one warning pattern instead of two, which reduces the number of insects killed in the learning process.

Nevertheless, there are cases where stealth is the motivation. Thick-headed flies mimic certain wasps, and visit the same flowers, in order to get close enough to lay their eggs on the wasps in order to parasitize them. Certain rove beetles mimic not only the shape of ants but also some of the chemicals used by the ants for recognition purposes. They can thus gain entry to ants' nests, where they prey on eggs and larvae. They are even fed by the ants!

The mud-dauber will often enter, and build its nests in, human habitation.

The cotton stainer's striking colour pattern tells of its distastefulness.

On yellow fls of
Deverra aphylla
(Cham.& Schlechtd.)
DC. (Apiaceae)

CA
Ge
Nol
NNE Twee Rivieren,
8-11.iii.1990
F.W. & S.K.Gess

Par
Gi
det.F.W.Gess.90.

# COLLECTING INSECTS

Collecting insects can be a hugely enjoyable pastime – and a very worthwhile one: many scientific studies rely on information extracted from collections of both the museum and private kind. The one that you begin building up in the privacy of your home can therefore, at some point, make a real contribution to the body of knowledge on our insect fauna.

There are a number of publications on the bookshelves that cover the subject in some detail (see Further Reading, page 85). The following is a brief summary of the fundamentals.

## Catching insects

**THE MANUAL APPROACH** The most basic item in your toolkit is the insect net, a simple piece of equipment that can easily be made at home. The bag, which consists of mosquito netting or a similar see-through material, should be tapered, its length just over twice the diameter of the opening (this allows the handle to be twisted to fold the bag over the rim, so that the insects you capture cannot escape). The bag is attached, by means of a band of stronger material, to a sturdy circular wire frame about 400 mm in diameter and fitted with a handle. The latter can be improvised – from a broomstick, for example, or aluminium tubing – and should be about 700 mm long, though this may be varied according to your particular preferences. Some commercially available nets have extendible handles.

**Above**: A standard insect net (right), a sweep net (left) and a beating tray (centre). **Opposite page:** A small wasp mounted, on a stage, with the use of a minuten pin; note the informative labels.
**Below:** A typical soldier fly.

For the most part, nets are designed for flying insects but a reinforced version, with a bag made from stronger material, can be used to sweep the tops of low-growing vegetation and grass. This type is called a sweep net. Aquatic insects are caught by drawing a suitable net through the water at the vegetated edge of a pond or dam.

An additional item, useful for collecting insects from tree foliage, is the beating tray. Made from cloth stretched over a frame and with a short handle, the tray is held below the foliage and the branch is tapped sharply with a heavy stick or wooden mallet in order to dislodge the insects.

**TRAPS** There are literally dozens of ways of trapping insects, each intended to take advantage of one or more aspects of their behaviour. They can be just as selective as you want them to be: there is plenty of scope to devise just the kind of traps that will catch those species you are especially interested in.

One option is the Malaise trap, designed for a wide range of day-flying insects (see also Further Reading, page 85). The trap, part of which is a vertical sheet of netting, is set across an insect path through perhaps forest or a gap between bushes. Insects flying into it will crawl upwards, and are finally led, by the slope of the roof, into a container holding either 70 per cent alcohol or a killing agent such as dichlorvos. Alcohol is really suitable only for insects such as bees, wasps and beetles; dichlorvos is preferable for flies and similar insects, though the container should be cleared frequently as specimens tend to dry out. Butterflies killed by either method generally make poor specimens.

Ground-living insects, such as ants and various kinds of beetles, can be collected in pitfall traps, which can be made from any suitably-sized jar or tin. These are set in the ground, with their rims flush with the surface, and half filled with water laced with a few drops of detergent. The specimens should be removed quickly, before they start to rot. Vertical baffles placed around the trap will improve its efficiency.

Pitfall traps rely on the chance passage of insects, though they can be fairly selective if baited. For dung beetles, for example, simply set a small bucket containing sand and fresh dung in the ground, and cover the top with stiff gauze cut crosswise by two slits (to allow the beetles to enter, and making escape difficult). A more complex arrangement is an empty bucket fitted with a funnel, the whole surmounted by a gauze-covered bowl containing dung.

Fermenting fruit will attract chafers and other fruit-eating beetles. Butterflies of the family Charaxidae and some others, mainly from the family Nymphalidae, will readily enter a special net trap baited with overripe bananas.

Light traps are very effective for a wide variety of nocturnal flying insects. But they all involve containers in which the insects accumulate and, even if a killing agent is used, delicate specimens such as moths are often damaged by the activities of the more robust captives. An alternative is to hang a bright light, preferably rich in ultra violet (such as a mercury vapour lamp), in front of a white sheet suspended from a branch and extending onto the ground. If no electricity is available a gas lamp, of the type used for camping, is a good substitute. Specimens are picked off the sheet as they arrive.

An underwater light trap, consisting of a waterproof torch at the end of a gauze cylinder fitted with a gauze funnel, will attract a wide range of aquatic insects.

**Above:** The vertical vanes around this pitfall trap extend its collecting area and guide the insects into the container. **Top right:** A light trap – among the most efficient ways of collecting nocturnal insects.

Trap-nests set in a tree.

Trap-nests fitted with windows enable you to observe the insects' nesting habits.

**TRAP-NESTS** These are artificial homes for bees and wasps that nest in natural cavities. The simplest ones comprise bundles of short bamboo lengths (with bores ranging from about 5 to 15 mm) that are closed at one end and attached to branches of trees and bushes, or even to the roof beams of buildings. Once they are filled with nest cells they can be stored until the adults of the next generation, or their parasites, emerge. During the earlier stages you can split them open to see what the immatures look like and how the cells are being provisioned, but in doing so the nest is more or less destroyed and the occupants may well die. Rather, fit the trap-nests with windows to allow you leisurely observation of the insects' nesting habits.

## Killing the specimens

A fairly small killing jar, perhaps a glass spice or mustard container, is quite suitable for dispatching most insects, though a second, larger one can be useful for the odd, very large specimen. Ideally the jar should be closed with a cork, but a tight-fitting screw top will do. If the lid is of plastic it must be the type that remains unaffected by ethyl acetate, the safest and most effective killing agent.

Prepare the jar by placing a little cotton wool at the bottom and pour in plaster of Paris to give a thickness of about 10 to 20 mm.

Before the plaster sets, make a few small holes in it to allow ethyl acetate to soak into the cotton wool underneath. The fumes of the acetate, which remain active for quite a few days, will kill most insects quickly. Larger beetles, though, may require at least 12 hours' exposure. A piece of toilet tissue helps keep specimens apart from each other and soaks up excess moisture.

Because their wings are fragile, butterflies demand different treatment: pinch the thorax between thumb and forefinger, though not so hard as to damage the specimen. With practice, you will learn the exact amount of pressure required. You can then place the insect in the killing jar to make sure (though this is seldom necessary), but see that the latter doesn't hold too much ethyl acetate liquid: the specimen will be spoiled if its wings become wet. Keep separate jars for butterflies and moths.

Specimens can be left in the jar: as long as it contains ethyl acetate they will remain soft and suitable for pinning. This may not be feasible on extended collecting trips because your jars will

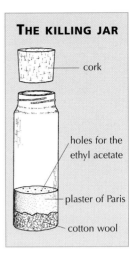

**THE KILLING JAR**

- cork
- holes for the ethyl acetate
- plaster of Paris
- cotton wool

soon become too full, in which case place the specimens in folded tissues packed in an air-tight container holding a small quantity of chlorocresol crystals. Keep the contents damp by adding a few drops of water now and again. Thus stored, the insect bodies will remain in a relaxed state for weeks and even months.

## Pinning

Correct and careful pinning is a vital part of the collecting process, for both aesthetic and practical reasons: well displayed, the specimens will look attractive, and be easier to examine and compare. Use proper insect pins, which are longer than ordinary ones and will not corrode. They are available in a range of thicknesses to suit different insect sizes.

Insects of more than about 8 mm in length, and which do not need to have their wings spread out, are pinned directly on boards of paper-covered polystyrene to dry. Precisely where the pin is inserted through the specimen depends on the insect order, and is dictated by a convention which ensures that features valuable to identification are not obscured (see box below).

Antennae, legs and wings are arranged in as lifelike a way as possible and held in position with further pins until they have dried out and stiffened. The specimens should be at a uniform height on their pins, with enough room left below for attaching one or more labels after removing them from the board and transferring them to your collection.

Butterflies, moths, dragonflies, antlions and other insects that need to have their wings spread are pinned on a setting board, with a groove running down its centre to accommodate their bodies. The wings are moved into place using pins and held in position with strips of paper. Conventionally, the wings of butterflies and moths are arranged so that the rear edges of both forewings form a straight line.

Very small insects are fixed with miniature pins, known as minuten pins, which are passed through small strips of polystyrene or cardboard. These in turn are mounted, together with their labels, on normal pins.

Specimens too small even for minuten pins can be fixed to small cardboard stages with tiny amounts of paper glue.

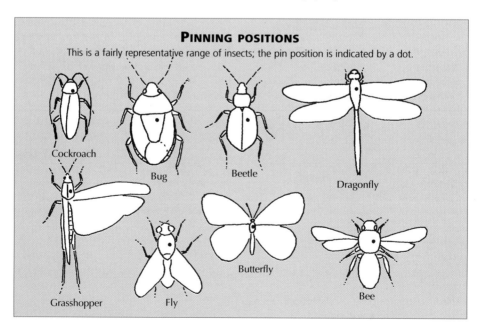

### PINNING POSITIONS
This is a fairly representative range of insects; the pin position is indicated by a dot.

Cockroach

Bug

Beetle

Dragonfly

Grasshopper

Fly

Butterfly

Bee

Soft-bodied insects, such as termites, caterpillars and other larvae, should be preserved in 70 per cent alcohol in well-sealed bottles or vials. These should be identified by labels, written in waterproof Indian ink or pencil.

## Labelling

Correct labelling is also extremely important if your collection is to have any scientific value. Each label must specify exactly where the insect was caught. Note down the latitude and longitude, in degrees and minutes, to avoid possible confusion with other localities of the same name. The information should

also give the date, and the collector's name. A second label, placed below the main one, may carry information about habitat, what the insect was doing, how it was collected and anything else of significance.

## Storing insects

Once a specimen is dry it will be brittle and easily damaged, but will nevertheless last indefinitely just so long as it is carefully protected, especially from pests such as museum beetles. You will need an insect-proof, preferably air-tight drawer or box with a sealed lid. The latter should if possible be of glass so that your collection can be viewed without having to open the container. Place an insect repellent

such as naphthalene (moth balls), paradichlorbenzene or camphor blocks, or small blocks of dichlorvos (commercially available as Vapona strips), inside and renew as required.

Line the storage container with paper-covered cork, polystyrene or, ideally, a high-density foam material (this is commercially available as EPX) which does not need covering with paper and holds the pins firmly.

The simplest arrangement is to have the specimens in rows, suitably grouped according to species, but this does have its disadvantages: once a container is full, the whole collection has to be rearranged if additional specimens of a particular species are to be accommodated. So consider the unit tray system of small, movable cardboard boxes of various sizes that neatly fit together in the container. Typically, each tray houses a single species, so that the collection remains flexible: it can be expanded without having to move individual specimens around. Only the trays are handled.

## Tailpiece

We hope this book has stimulated your interest to the point of wanting to learn more about insects. And what better way to do this than to start a collection? Quite apart from the scientific value it may have, it will provide you with an absorbing hobby. You may start by collecting all kinds of specimens, but as you continue to observe the insect world your interest will no doubt focus on a group you find especially fascinating. You will never regret the time so spent, and the chances are that insects will provide you with a life-long source of enjoyment – if not a rewarding career.

**Above:** The conventional and unit tray systems of storing and displaying insects **Top centre:** Insects drying on a pinning board; butterflies on a grooved setting board.

# GLOSSARY

**alate:** Winged form of ant and termite, and any other insect that also has wingless forms.

**carnivorous:** Flesh-eating or feeding on other animals.

**caste:** Category of mature individual found among social insects, such as queen, soldier, worker, alate.

**cerci:** Paired appendages at end of abdomen, usually filamentous and segmented.

**chitin:** Substance from which hard parts of insect bodies are made.

**cocoon:** A covering or case consisting mostly of silk spun by the larvae of many insects as protection for the pupa.

**compound eyes:** The large lateral eyes found on most insects, each made up of many separate visual elements.

**coxa:** Basal segment of the leg by which it is articulated with the body.

**cuticle:** Outer covering of an insect, made from chitin.

**diurnal:** Flying or otherwise active during the day.

**dorsal:** The upper surface or back.

**elongate:** Lengthened, extended or drawn out.

**elytra:** Hardened forewings of beetles, which act as covers for the hindwings when at rest.

**endemic:** Occurring naturally only in a given region.

**femur:** The third section of an insect leg.

**frass:** Solid faecal pellets or droppings (excrement) produced by insects.

**granivorous:** Feeding on grain or seeds.

**haemocoel:** Body cavity of an insect, in which the blood circulates.

**haemolymph:** Blood of insects and other lower invertebrates.

**haltere:** Small club-shaped balancing organs, one found on each side of the thorax of flies (Diptera) in place of the hindwings from which they are derived.

**hemimetabolous:** Insects which undergo an incomplete metamorphosis.

**herbivorous:** Feeding on plant tissue.

**holometabolous:** Insects which undergo complete metamorphosis with clearly differentiated larval, pupal and adult stages.

**hypermetamorphosis:** Unusually complex metamorphosis with a number of different larval stages.

**larva:** Young stage of those insects which undergo complete metamorphosis; they bear no resemblance to the adult.

**Malpighian tubules:** Blind excretory tubes that open into the beginning of the hind intestine.

**metamorphosis:** The change that occurs during the development of an insect from young to adult.

**myiasis:** Disease or injury caused by the attack of fly (Diptera) larvae.

**naiad:** Aquatic larva of some hemimetabolous insects that bear no resemblance to the adults, for instance the young of dragonflies, damselflies and mayflies.

**neopterous:** The ability to fold the wings over the back when at rest.

**nocturnal:** Flying or otherwise active during the night.

**nymph:** The young stage of insects which undergo incomplete metamorphosis (exopterygota). Nymphs have the same feeding habits as, and are more or less similar to, the adults.

**ocelli:** Simple eyes (as opposed to compound).

**omnivorous:** Feeding on a wide variety of animal and vegetable material.

**ostia:** Slit-like openings of the insect heart.

**ovipositor:** A structure used for laying eggs.

**palaeopterous:** Inability to fold the wings over the back when at rest.

**parasitoid:** An internal or external parasite that usually causes the death of its host.

**pharynx:** A slightly enlarged section of the alimentary canal at the beginning of the oesophagus (the back part of the mouth and upper part of the throat).

**pheromone:** A chemical secreted externally in minute quantities, and which may attract the opposite sex or, in social insects, regulate various activities in the nest or hive.

**proboscis:** Extended, elongate mouth structure.

**pronotum:** Upper surface of the front segment of the thorax (prothorax).

**pupa:** The usually inactive stage between larva and adult in insects which undergo complete metamorphosis; pupae do not feed.

**ringbark:** To cut the bark around a branch, killing off the limb above the cut.

**sclerotin:** Alternative term for chitin.

**seta/ae:** Hairs and scales connected to the cuticle by a membranous joint.

**spermatheca:** A receptacle within the female that receives and stores sperm from the male.

**spermatophore:** A capsule or packet containing sperm.

**spiracles:** Openings along the sides of the insect body through which air enters the tracheae.

**sternum:** The cuticle on the lower (ventral) side of each segment.

**stridulation:** The production of sound by rubbing together various parts of the body.

**substrate:** The surface on which an object (an insect) is resting.

**tarsus:** The fifth and terminal section of the insect leg, jointed and with claws.

**tergum:** The cuticle on the upper (dorsal) side of each segment.

**tibia:** The fourth section of the insect leg.

**tracheae:** Tubes that ramify through the insect body, conducting air to the tissues.

**tracheoles:** Fine cellular tubules through whose walls gases diffuse into the tissues.

**trochanter:** The second section of the insect leg.

# FURTHER READING

Annecke, DP and Moran, VC. *Insects and Mites of Cultivated Plants in South Africa*. Butterworths, Durban.

Attenborough, D. 1980. *Life on Earth*. Reader's Digest Association, London.

Braack, LEO. 1991. *Field Guide to the Insects of the Kruger National Park*. Struik Publishers, Cape Town.

Butler, CG. 1954. *The World of the Honeybee*. Collins, London.

Clark, GC and Dickson, CGC. 1971. *Life Histories of the South African Lycaenid Butterflies*. Purnell, Cape Town.

Dirsh, VM. 1965. *The African Genera of Acridoidea*. Cambridge University Press, Cambridge.

Evans, HE and O'Neill, KM. 1988. *The Natural History and Behavior of North American Beewolves*. Comstock Publishing Associates, Ithaca.

Evans, HE and West-Eberhard, MJ. 1970. *The Wasps*. University of Michigan Press.

Frost, SW. 1959. *Insect Life and Insect Natural History*. Dover Publications, New York.

Gauld, I and Bolton, B. 1988. *The Hymenoptera*. Oxford University Press, Oxford.

Gess, SK. 1996. *The Pollen Wasps*. Harvard University Press, Cambridge, Massachusetts.

Halffter, G and Edmonds, WD. 1982. *The Nesting Behavior of Dung Beetles* (Scarabaeinae). Instituto de Ecologia, Mexico.

Holldobler, B and Wilson, EO. 1994. *Journey to the Ants*. Belknap Press, Cambridge, Massachusetts.

Holm, E. and de Meillon, E. 1995. *Pocket Guide to Insects of Southern Africa*. Struik Publishers, Cape Town.

Holm, E. 1986. *Insects*. Struik Publishers, Cape Town.

Lovegrove, B. 1993. *The Living Deserts of Southern Africa*. Fernwood Press, Vlaeberg.

McGavin, GC. 1993. *Bugs of the World*. Blandford, London.

Oldroyd, H. 1958. *Collecting, Preserving and Studying Insects*. Hutchinson, London.

Oldroyd, H. 1974. 'An Introduction to the Robber Flies (Diptera: Asilidae) of South Africa'. *Annals of the Natal Museum*, 22(1): 1-171.

O'Toole, C. 1995. *Alien Empire*. BBC Books, London.

O'Toole, C. and Preston-Mafham, K. 1985. *Insects in Camera*. Oxford University Press, Oxford.

Pinhey, ECG. 1962. *Hawk Moths of Central and Southern Africa*. Longmans, Cape Town.

Pinhey, ECG. 1972. *Emperor Moths of South and South Central Africa*. Struik Publishers, Cape Town

Pinhey, ECG. 1975. *Moths of Southern Africa*. Tafelberg Publishers Ltd, Cape Town.

Preston-Mafham, K. 1990. *Grasshoppers and Mantids of the World*. Blandford, London.

Price, PW. 1975. *Insect Ecology*. John Wiley & Sons, New York.

Pringle, ELL, Henning, GA and Ball, JB. (Eds). 1994. *Pennington's Butterflies of Southern Africa*. Struik Winchester, Cape Town.

Richards, OW and Davies, RG. 1977. *Imm's General Textbook of Entomology*. 10th edition. Chapman and Hall, London.

Ross, KG and Matthews, RW. 1991. *The Social Biology of Wasps*. Comstock Publishing Associates, Ithaca.

Roubik, DW. 1989. *Ecology and Natural History of Tropical Bees*. Cambridge University Press, Cambridge.

Sbordoni, V. and Forestiero, S. 1985. *The World of Butterflies*. Blandford Press, Poole, Dorset.

Scholtz, CH. 1984. *Useful Insects*. Insight Series. De Jager-HAUM, Pretoria.

Scholtz, CH and Holm, E. 1985. *Insects of Southern Africa*. Butterworths, Durban.

Seely, M. 1987. *The Namib – Natural History of an Ancient Desert*. Shell Oil SWA Ltd, Windhoek.

Skaife, SH. 1955. *Dwellers in Darkness*. Longmans, London.

Skaife, SH. 1979 (revised edition). *African Insect Life*. C. Struik, Cape Town.

Smit, B. 1964. *Insects in Southern Africa – How to Control Them*. Oxford University Press, Cape Town.

Smith, KGV. 1973. *Insects and Other Arthropods of Medical Importance*. Trustees of the British Museum (Natural History), London.

Spoczynska, JOI. 1975. *The World of the Wasp*. Frederick Muller Ltd, London.

Townes, H. 1972. 'A light-weight Malaise trap.' *Entomological News* 83: 239-247.

Werger, MJA. 1978. *Biogeography and Ecology of Southern Africa*. Dr W. Junk bv Publishers, The Hague.

West, L and Ridl, J. 1994. *How to Photograph Insects and Spiders*. Stackpole Books, Mechanicsburg, Pennsylvania.

Wigglesworth, VB. 1964. *The Life of Insects*. Weidenfeld and Nicolson, London.

Wilson, EO. 1971. *The Insect Societies*. Belknap Press, Cambridge, Massachusetts.

# PICTURE CREDITS

# INDEX

Page numbers in Italics indicate illustrations.

*Southern African Insects and their World* illuminates the infinitely varied, often colourful, always fascinating array of arthropods – bugs, butterflies, beetles and other six-legged creatures – that inhabit southern Africa.

The book is divided into an introductory overview and seven thematic chapters that describe, in easy-to-understand text complemented by illustrations and by a wealth of full-colour photographs, the physical nature of insects, the various groups into which they are classified, their mating and breeding habits, their search for food and their fight for survival. A special section is devoted to the social insects – colonial termites, bees, wasps and ants – that have perfected the art of communal living and which, in many instances, rank among Nature's finest architects. The final chapter covers the basic do's and don'ts of building up a home insect collection.

**Alan Weaving** is a respected entomologist who worked in Kenya, Zimbabwe and Honduras before returning to South Africa to join the Albany Museum in Grahamstown, where he specialized in the behaviour of solitary wasps. He is now retired. A keen and much-published photographer of natural history, he has travelled widely in southern and East Africa in search of subjects.

ISBN 1-86872-320-8

9 781868 723201